T0034398

BY WARREN ZANES

Dusty in Memphis

Revolutions in Sound: Warner Bros. Records

Petty: The Biography

Deliver Me from Nowhere

Runnin' Down a Dream: Tom Petty and the Heartbreakers
    (editor)

Waiting for a Train: Jimmie Rodgers's America (co-editor)

DELIVER
ME
FROM
NOWHERE

DELIVER ME FROM NOWHERE

The Making of Bruce Springsteen's *Nebraska*

WARREN ZANES

CROWN

NEW YORK

2024 Crown Trade Paperback Edition

Copyright © 2023 by Warren Zanes

All rights reserved.

Published in the United States by Crown, an imprint of the Crown Publishing Group, a division of Penguin Random House LLC, New York.

CROWN and the Crown colophon are registered trademarks of Penguin Random House LLC.

Originally published in hardcover in the United States by Crown, an imprint of Crown Publishing Group, a division of Penguin Random House LLC, in 2023.

Grateful acknowledgment is made to Sony Music Publishing (US) LLC for permission to reprint excerpts from: "Nebraska" (Bruce Springsteen), copyright © 1982 by Sony Music Publishing (US) LLC and Eldridge Publishing Co., and "Mansion on the Hill," copyright © 1982 by Sony Music Publishing (US) LLC and Eldridge Publishing Co. All rights are administered by Sony Music Publishing (US) LLC, 424 Church Street, Suite 1200, Nashville, TN 37219.

LIBRARY OF CONGRESS CATALOGING-IN-PUBLICATION DATA
Names: Zanes, Warren, author.
Title: Deliver me from nowhere / Warren Zanes.
Description: First edition. | New York: Crown, 2023.
Identifiers: LCCN 2022052300 (print) | LCCN 2022052301 (ebook) | ISBN 9780593237434 (tradepaper) | ISBN 9780593237427 (ebook)
Subjects: LCSH: Springsteen, Bruce. Nebraska. | Popular music—United States—1981–1990—History and criticism.
Classification: LCC ML420.S77 Z35 2923 (print) | LCC ML420.S77 (ebook) | DDC 782.42164092—dc23/eng/20221103
LC record available at https://lccn.loc.gov/2022052300

Printed in the United States of America on acid-free paper

crownpublishing.com

9 8 7 6 5 4 3 2 1

Book design by Caroline Cunningham

For Lucian and Piero, always

It was a house that's five minutes up the street from here. Just down a little lane, a little one-level ranch house. It had '70s shag carpet, orange, wall-to-wall. The bedroom was just a tiny room off the reservoir. It was kind of a funky place where I'd be staying for a year or so after I came in off the road. I'd lost my farmhouse that I'd lived in, where I'd written *Darkness* and *The River,* and this was right after that. I was basically interested in not spending tons of time in the studio trying to see if I had recordable material. So I told Mike [Batlan] I need some sort of home taping setup that'd allow me to overdub, something just a little better than the thing I'd usually sing my songs into. He went out and got the TEAC four-track cassette player. That's kinda how it happened.

—Bruce Springsteen, speaking to the author, Colts Neck, N.J., 2021

CONTENTS

SUGGESTED RESOURCES

Terrence Malick's *Badlands*

Suicide's "Frankie Teardrop"

Hank Mizell's "Jungle Rock"

Charles Laughton's *The Night of the Hunter*

Flannery O'Connor's "A Good Man Is Hard to Find" and "Good Country People"

Hank Williams's "A Mansion on the Hill"

Robert Frank's *The Americans*

Bruce Springsteen's first seven studio recordings

DELIVER
ME
FROM
NOWHERE

PROLOGUE

The Rhinoceros Club

We were sitting in the cramped dressing room at the back of the Rhinoceros Club in Greensboro, North Carolina, a little place on South Greene Street across from the Carolina Theatre. It was January 17, 1985. Since we were due to go onstage in ten or fifteen minutes, the drinking had picked up. I was in my late teens at the time, a kid guitar player in a rock and roll band called the Del Fuegos. The club, about a hundred-person capacity, was probably half-full. Not bad for a cold night in the mid-South. Our itinerary would take us farther down the Eastern Seaboard, then west, one small rock club to the next, until winter was behind us. But the palm trees were weeks away. We were writing out a set list for the show when Nils Lofgren came in the dressing room door.

Bruce Springsteen and the E Street Band were on tour, taking a night off between shows in Charlotte and Greensboro. *Born in the U.S.A.* was on its third single of seven, the title track, "Born in the U.S.A." Calling the album "a triumph" had become something of a reflex among critics. Of course, if you grew up in the Northeast, as most of my band had, "triumph" seemed like Bruce's native territory. But, yes, this one was bigger. Even Bruce's body had changed, as if in response to it all. He had muscles.

Excited to have Nils Lofgren there with us, we asked him to come onstage for a few songs, handed him one of our backup guitars, and suggested "In the Midnight Hour" in the key of E. And that's about when the door opened again and Bruce Springsteen walked in. "I got your album," Springsteen said as he came into the room, " 'Backseat Nothing' is my favorite song." He spoke before we could. Then we couldn't.

Minutes later, Springsteen was leading us through a few sloppy rock and roll classics, "Hang On Sloopy" and "Stand By Me." He can't be blamed for the sloppiness. We brought that. But he knew the place and was generous enough to go back there to meet us. He stretched the songs out, let some joy flood the room, made a few people reconsider the possibility of small-town miracles. There was only one pay phone in the Rhinoceros Club, but word got out fast. By the time Springsteen finally exited the stage and went into the night, with a little help from some security, the room was probably three times its legal capacity. For the next two years, every interview we did started with the same question: "What was it like to play with Bruce Springsteen?"

We'd just put out that first record of ours, were still searching for some idea of who we were and what, if anything, we had to contribute to the great, many-voiced conversation/argument of rock and roll, and one of our heroes happened to walk into the club on South Greene Street where we were playing. In that moment in American life, it seemed you couldn't turn on a radio without hearing Bruce Springsteen or buy a magazine without seeing him. But that wasn't what mattered to us. Not right then. It wasn't even the earlier records like *Born to Run* or *Darkness on the Edge of Town* that were on our minds, though we knew them line for line. When our dressing room door opened and Bruce Springsteen walked in, we had one thought: that's the guy who made *Nebraska*.

INTRODUCTION

The King of Pop and the Beer Can

A few weeks after getting onstage at Greensboro's Rhinoceros Club, Bruce Springsteen wrapped up the first leg of the *Born in the U.S.A.* North American tour. The final show was in Syracuse, January 27, 1985, some fifty thousand people in attendance. Having completed more than ninety shows and needing the break, Springsteen nonetheless got on a plane the day after the show and headed for A&M Studios in Los Angeles. There he'd participate in the USA for Africa recording being produced by Quincy Jones.

Springsteen flew commercial, then grabbed a rental car at the airport. He wasn't an entourage kind of guy. Rosanne Cash would later describe watching Springsteen walk unnoticed through a large crowd of New York City tourists, using only a hoodie. "It's my invisibility cloak," he told her. He knew how to get around. When it came to Los Angeles, the city was a second home of sorts. LAX was a breeze. It was an easy, familiar drive from there to the A&M lot.

They were valet-parking cars at A&M. One of the attendants handling the operation was a top record executive willing to do some honest work if that was his only way to be a part of the evening. Husbands and wives, boyfriends, girlfriends, and children: none were allowed into the studio where the recording would happen. Steve Perry from Journey, first to come and last to leave, had already found a spot for himself in the control room when Springsteen was still on his way from the airport. He was watching Quincy Jones record Michael Jackson's vocal part, asking no one in particular, "Am I on drugs?" Springsteen, before getting to the valet parking, found a good spot on La Brea. It was something he couldn't resist. He parked on the street and walked by foot to the studio, passing the office inside the gate that had once belonged to Charlie Chaplin.

The list of artists who showed up that night was striking. Still is. Willie Nelson, Diana Ross, Bob Dylan, Stevie Wonder, Dionne Warwick, Ray Charles, Tina Turner, Billy Joel, Paul Simon, Bette Midler, Kenny Rogers, Steve Perry, Cyndi Lauper, Al Jarreau. There were others. Michael Jackson and Lionel Richie wrote the song they'd be singing. Historically speaking, it was the largest gathering of star power ever to come together in a recording studio to perform what most of them believed was a terrible song.

"I don't think anybody liked it," Billy Joel recalled. Cyndi Lauper is reported to have described it as "a Pepsi commercial." How did it all come together? As Ryan D'Agostino would later recount in *Esquire,* the organizing was a matter of making a lot of calls . . . until Bruce Springsteen agreed to participate. "Bruce was in. Everybody wanted in."

Michael Jackson, mostly quiet throughout a session that went all night, saw Springsteen's empty Budweiser can and asked someone to take his picture with it. When Michael Jackson is getting his photo taken with your beer can, you could say things are going well career-wise.

Born in the U.S.A. was like a light shined directly in the eyes. It overwhelmed everything else. For all the glory and hard work of Springsteen's career, in 1985 there would be vast parts of the audience who didn't know the prehistory. The fabled beginnings—a record deal reportedly signed on a car hood with Columbia's legendary A&R man John Hammond, the celebrated *Born to Run,* a young man who was on the covers of *Time* and *Newsweek* the very same week—the new fans would find out about all that over time. But just then they saw the guy in a video dancing with what appeared to be an underage girl, singing "Dancing in the Dark." He wasn't even holding a guitar. It wasn't just Ronald Reagan who mistook Springsteen for another man, though Reagan did it most publicly when he aligned himself with "Born in the U.S.A.," touting Springsteen as a man who understood Reagan's kind of American values. People were getting shit wrong.

"The aftermath of the *Born in the U.S.A.* tour," Springsteen wrote in *Born to Run,* "was a strange time. It was the peak of something. I would never be here, this high, in the mainstream pop firmament again. It was the end of something." While others might bask in such a moment, Springsteen saw it all differently, as the "end of something." One thing that was obscured in it all was the album that came before *Born in the U.S.A.*: *Nebraska*. Of all his albums, it was the furthest from *Born in the U.S.A.* It was also the very thing that allowed *Born in the U.S.A.* to come into being.

———

Nebraska had something of a time-release quality. It revealed its strange power over the years, a thing people found in their own way and on their own time. It was passed around like a rumor. Artists of different kinds would still be tapping *Nebraska's* meaning years after its initial release. I interviewed several musicians and songwriters for this book, some who heard *Nebraska* when it came out, some who would find it later. I wanted to know their *Nebraska*s. Patty Griffin, Steve Earle, Richard Thompson, Rosanne Cash, and others. Most of them I knew from playing shows or working on documentaries. Their thoughts would infuse my own as I searched through the layers of *Nebraska*. They became a part of this book.

The lead singer of the National, Matt Berninger, was one of those artists. "*Born in the U.S.A.* was my first experience, really," he told me. "I think I was thirteen when it came out. My sister was just starting Columbia House, the mail-order thing—you know, *eight CDs for a penny!*—so she was buying tons of stuff. The Smiths, U2. *Born in the U.S.A.* was one of them."

Berninger was no different from so many others of his generation, tuned in to MTV, listening to terrestrial radio, borrowing an older sibling's music, absorbing all that he could. Springsteen, Prince, Madonna, the giants of the time, were seemingly omnipresent, blown up to an unprecedented scale through the increased visuality of popular culture. One day, though, Berninger would be on a stage with his own group, covering "Mansion on the Hill" from Springsteen's *Nebraska* album.

"I didn't actually hear *Nebraska* until a couple of years after hearing *Born in the U.S.A.*," he went on, "maybe freshman year in college. But out of sequence. That's when I think I was like, *there's more to Bruce Springsteen than this cultural giant I'm seeing.* I mean, *Born in the U.S.A.* was this Madonna-level thing. The discovery of a record like *Nebraska,* after the ubiquity and endless singles of *Born in the U.S.A.,* was particularly striking." In the process of taking in the superstars of his adolescence and then learning that some of them, like Prince, had prehistories, Berninger also learned that there was only one artist with a record like *Nebraska. Nebraska* wasn't some obscurity from an earlier point in the artist's career, a collection of outtakes or relics, nothing like that. It was Springsteen's sixth official release, the follow-up to his first number one album, *The River.*

"To hear Bruce Springsteen in such an intimate way, no drums, very simple instrumentation, was surprising," Berninger recalled. "It was like, 'What? What is this? Can you *do* this?' It wasn't just the fact that it was a magical record in terms of its scenes and characters. It was the idea that a major rock star could make something just in his bedroom. It exploded so many of my received ideas and told me that, maybe . . . maybe I could be a musician." Berninger wasn't the only one who took it that way. However different in scale and effect, *Nebraska* did for some what the Beatles' appearance on *The Ed Sullivan*

Show in 1964 did for so many at that time. It said, "You can do this."

"I think *Nebraska* set so many bands on their way," Berninger insisted. "Every band that went after a lo-fi, DIY kind of thing. Pavement, Silver Jews, Guided by Voices, all the early indie stuff. I think *Nebraska* was the big bang of the indie rock that was about making shit alone in your bedroom. It's like when Justin Vernon made *For Emma, Forever Ago*. I'm sure he was trying to make his version of *Nebraska* when he did that. And he did. Justin Vernon's record changed the landscape. That project is a child of *Nebraska*."

WZ: After finishing *Nebraska,* you said you felt it was your best work.

SPRINGSTEEN: Yeah, I felt that it was. Still may be.

Nebraska is the recording that matters the most in Bruce Springsteen's career, but not because of the hits it contains or its renown or because a generation of young people played it on repeat while they searched for themselves in bedroom mirrors. It needs a different measure. Springsteen made the record when he was the object of tremendous expectations. At times it almost seemed as if rock and roll were his responsibility. MTV, the emerging digital technologies, the pervasive conservatism of the early 1980s: all seemed to be moving in a direction that had less and less to do with rock and roll's original, reckless spirit. It made a kind of sense to hold up Springsteen as the conscience and captain of all that was at risk. Fans, fellow artists, and critics were watching to see what he'd do in the wake of *The River,* an album that delivered Springsteen to his highest station yet. Really, they were waiting for *Born in the U.S.A.* And that's not what they got.

The truth was that Springsteen was a little lost. He was only a matter of months from a breakdown that he'd speak of very candidly decades later. The role he'd been given as a public figure was at odds with what he was experiencing behind the image he'd created. He went into a solitude that was more powerful than he was himself. But, always a worker, when he was there, he recorded music. The rarest part of that experience, however, was that he released it. That move went against his original intentions, what any record company would hope for as a follow-up to *The River,* and the expectations of his fans. This was the record he did for himself, without even knowing he was making a record. As his manager, Jon Landau, said to me, "If you listen to that vocal style on *Nebraska,* it's different from any other record. It's like he's singing to himself."

Nebraska would become a reference point for people who write songs and record them, a reminder that you can strip off all the wallpaper, tear out the drywall, take it down to the studs. And probably every now and then you should. When *Nebraska* was first released, and because no one knew what was going on with Springsteen, it looked to some like an act of defiance. To others it seemed a terrible career choice. There were people who loved it for both reasons, and my old band was among them. *Nebraska* seemed to take up some of punk rock's unfinished business, which was substantial.

Acts that were born into or at least corralled into the punk category, whether the Clash or, more distantly, the Police, seemed to be getting bigger and bigger in the early 1980s, and friendlier and friendlier with radio, stadiums, charts. It seemed inevitable that these groups would achieve that success, and while there was no reason to begrudge them such an outcome, it was making it harder to see their connections to punk thought and action. Then *Nebraska* came along, a major release by a major artist, an album that was cutting deals with no one. It might not have sounded like punk rock, but it sure behaved like it.

The scurry to figure out what *Nebraska* was—it was Bruce Springsteen's follow-up to *The River*, so it was natural that there would be great interest—obscured the brute fact that this was one of popular music's most enigmatic moments. Ever. This wasn't an early version of the "Unplugged" phenomenon, which would involve artists on stools making beautifully re-corded versions of their hits without bringing a drummer to the gig. This was the sound of a man forcing out songs while held under water, a rough hand on his neck. He was poised to go big, then didn't. He all but went into hiding.

Really, with *Nebraska,* Springsteen set aside most of what seemed necessary for commercial success, from clean and clear fidelity to perfect performances to putting the artist's face on the album cover. He stripped so much away that, really, all that was left was the grunt of art. More than three decades later, the music writer Bryant Kitching described it as "punk as fuck."

In a time and place now remembered for its primary colors and pastels, as the moment when music television would begin to challenge the power of radio and Ronald Reagan would

soon speak of "Morning in America," *Nebraska* was an uniden-
tified species. It was a recording that had to be figured out,
more like a message from across time than another album
among the many released in 1982. That year had big winners
with Chicago's "Hard to Say I'm Sorry," the theme song from
Chariots of Fire, offerings from Foreigner, the J. Geils Band, the
Go-Go's, Asia, Men at Work.

Nebraska was made on a cassette four-track recorder, a TEAC
144, a relatively new technology that had been available to consumers for only three years at that point. The TEAC 144 was
primitive when compared with the gear in commercial studios,
but it signaled a shift: multitracking could be done at home,
and on a kind of tape you could buy at a record store, even a
CVS. But that didn't mean major artists were making their albums on the TEAC 144. They weren't.

Springsteen, an old pro at spending his allowance, per diem,
and salary on pay-by-the-day studios, got his 144 and, in one
deft move, cut the professional recording studio out of the creative process. While he intended no such thing, it was an act that
was prophetic in many ways. By the turn of the next century,
artists would regularly take to their bedrooms, kitchens, closets,
outhouses, wherever, to make their records. A great many recording studios would eventually close their doors for good
because of that migration. By that time, though, the TEAC
144 was a fossil, and home recording had entered the digital
age, just as rock and roll was no longer the reigning genre in
popular music.

In an article titled "How Bruce Springsteen's Nebraska
Sparked a Home Recording Revolution," Warren McQuiston

writes with unbridled joy recalling Springsteen's gesture and its liberating power:

> Imagine being one of those musicians starting out in the early 1980s and you've just spent a small fortune on recording equipment. You and your buddies have been playing around with this Portastudio, recording some stuff to try to hustle gigs or impress the guy/girl/guygirl you've been trying to talk to for weeks. And then the biggest fucking rock star on Earth releases an album that was made on the same beginner-level contraption with the red, white and green knobs you've got in your bedroom. You'd look at it a little differently, right? . . . The freaks had the keys! Underground music exploded; from Daniel Johnston to Ween to Neutral Milk Hotel to Iron & Wine to Bon Iver and on and on. It became the de facto home studio device in early hip-hop circles. . . . Think of your image of Springsteen and what he stands for. Shouldn't that be the guy to popularize a device that took the need for expensive studios away? He opened up the Myers Park Country Club for everybody.

But just then, in 1982, *Nebraska* wasn't simply an outcast when compared with the year's big hits; *Nebraska* didn't even make sense in relation to the sequence of Springsteen's *own* body of work, which conveyed some feeling of development and loosely planned if natural growth: *Greetings from Asbury Park, N.J.; The Wild, the Innocent & the E Street Shuffle; Born to Run; Darkness on the Edge of Town; The River*. Things had been building in one way or another, with the strong hint of a sequential story. Now this? *Nebraska*?

Nebraska was a cave painting in the age of photography. You had to crawl underground and through a few tight spaces to get at it. *Nebraska*'s production involved the absence of production. There's no producer credit on the album jacket. Because there *was* no production—short of the act of saying, "Just put out the demo." And not everyone involved agrees who said that first.

Like the National's Matt Berninger a few years later, my old band didn't know you could do what Springsteen had just done. It was unexpected enough, audacious enough, that we remember where we were when we first held it in our hands. *Nebraska*. Black and white and red. Those block letters.

Nebraska was imperfect, demanding in the sense of asking *too* much of the listener. Joel Selvin's original *San Francisco Chronicle* review put it thus: "It is a stark, raw document, rough edges intact, and so intimately personal it is surprising he would even play the tape for other people at all, let alone put it out as an album." There was no disclaimer on *Nebraska,* no defensive maneuvering, no "rarities" designation, no sticker explaining that these were demos cut quickly and at home. *Nebraska* was, simply, Bruce Springsteen's next album.

Thirty years later *The New Yorker* would describe the album's release as "a shock," using the same word that appeared in *Rolling Stone*'s original review. And while most shocking things become less shocking over time, this one hasn't. *Nebraska* was a move bold enough that you could appreciate it as an artistic act independent of your listening experience. Just the idea of it. In that sense, it was conceptual art. To put out as an official release these home recordings, rough sketches done in private and intended as nothing but an early draft of songs that would later be finalized and re-recorded "properly": that alone meant something.

Springsteen had been in bands for years, bumping against drum risers and leaning into microphones with guys he'd known since his teens. *The River* was a culmination of all that. With *The River*, Springsteen wanted to get on record the sound of his band, the experience of their show. "Of them all," he would say, "it's the album that most captures what happens when we play." But even when he was halfway through making it, something else was dogging Springsteen. He needed to go somewhere by himself. *Nebraska*. And, really, after he did go there, he never went back.

CHAPTER ONE

The First Question

Photography has something to do with resurrection.

—ROLAND BARTHES, *Camera Lucida*

In the spring of 2021, Bruce Springsteen invited me to spend some time with him in Colts Neck, New Jersey, so that we could talk about *Nebraska*. When I arrived, he walked out to my car to meet me. When it was all over, he walked me back out. Everything was hand delivered. I was wishing I'd parked three miles away. I'd grown up listening to the guy's records. I had a lot of questions, not all of which he should have to bother with.

Springsteen has lived with the joy and burden of people wanting his time. The intimacy of the music brings something out in people. He's probably had to scrape off hundreds of us just to stay on schedule. But that day I was his guest, and he was as good a host as I could ask for. He got me water to drink and then asked if I needed more. Later in the afternoon he wondered if coffee was a good idea. I was at the family house and—as I think we both understood—his responsibility. Any mess I made he'd have to clean up.

I wanted to know where *Nebraska* came from, what it led to. It sat between two of Springsteen's most celebrated recordings, in its own quiet and turmoil. He described it to me as "an accident start to finish" but also as the album that "still might be [his] best." The recording came from a place and a time in which Springsteen was facing troubles in his life, troubles that had no name as of yet. Wordsworth defines poetry as "the spontaneous overflow of powerful feelings . . . recollected in tranquillity." Quite differently, *Nebraska* came from the middle of that "overflow," was not a thing "recollected in tranquillity." It came from the heart of trouble and led to still more, its stark character the lasting reward.

Nebraska was unfinished, imperfect, delivered into a world hovering at the threshold of the digital, when technology would allow recorded music to hang itself on perfect time, carry perfect pitch, but also risk losing its connection to the unfixed and unfixable. Springsteen's manager, Jon Landau, recalled for me, over several afternoons at his Westchester home, the way in which *Nebraska* arrived. Chuck Plotkin, among Springsteen's producers and a key player in the last stages of *Nebraska*'s creation, would talk about the anxious labor of trying to make the album conform to industry standards. But Springsteen knew the most by far, because it came from his bedroom.

While we talked that day in Colts Neck, Patti Scialfa was recording next door. There were a few others around, but everyone left us alone. Patti was in the process of turning a song into a recording. For all the talk of the hours, the sweat, and the persistence involved in making records, it's worth remembering that the process is also among the highest forms of pleasure, particularly when you're watching your own song or one you love turn into the recording you feel it's meant to be . . . and it happens without complication. Any song could become a thousand different records, but sometimes the recording studio is a place of pure lightness because a song is becoming just the recording it should be. That afternoon in Colts Neck, you got the sense that things were going well in the studio next door.

But I was with Springsteen in another room, doing something very different. On one level, I was probing, asking about a time in his life that wasn't easy. Given the way Springsteen has interviewed throughout his career, it shouldn't have come as a surprise that he seemed to hold back nothing. Where he had no answer or a question of his own, he didn't pretend all knowingness. Some combination of an investment in the truth and what seemed genuine wonder made him an unguarded collaborator.

I'd been out to the Colts Neck house once before, on that occasion in my capacity as consulting producer on the documentary *Twenty Feet from Stardom*. The director, Morgan Neville, was conducting the interview that day and had a few pages of good questions. But I always remembered that Springsteen passed on the first of those questions, which surprised me. As a question it was a good opener, appropriate, well delivered. But Springsteen responded by saying something along the lines of "What else you got?"

Whether it was intended to or not, that response shifted the energy in the room. Frankly, I'd never seen an interview start like that. "What else you got?" The room belonged to Springsteen from that point forward. On the second question, he took a room of filmmakers who were slightly off axis to another place. He pictured the singers on Phil Spector recordings, including his friend Darlene Love, helped us hear and consider the youth in their voices. He'd obviously thought deeply about backup singers, the film's subject, and about the emotional layer those voices added to so many great recordings. This was a storyteller at work, not a Q&A session.

One story he told that day in Colts Neck revolved around his trip by Greyhound to a David Bowie session in Philadelphia, where Bowie was cutting two of Springsteen's songs. Bruce Springsteen was nobody at that point, just a weird name that suggested anything but what was coming. Luther Vandross, a key figure in *Twenty Feet from Stardom,* was at those same Bowie sessions, singing and arranging backups on Bowie's "Young Americans." The documentary's early edit already included some clips from that very session, with Luther Vandross leading the small vocal combo that added so much to "Young Americans." No one would have known that Bruce Springsteen lurked in the shadows, watching it go down. Pure coincidence. That is, no one knew Springsteen was there that day until he told the story at his Colts Neck home.

Twenty Feet from Stardom was given a fresh edit just after that interview. From that point forward the film opened with Springsteen. He was that good. But I'll tell you this, the experience made me consider at some length the first question I planned to ask during my *Nebraska* interview, on my second visit to Colts Neck. I just didn't want to hear him say, "What else you got?" I wasn't sure I had the backbone to hear that and still be ready for the next question. So I developed a foolproof method to avoid such a moment: make it a yes-or-no question.

> **WZ:** Are there any photographs of the room where you
>   recorded *Nebraska*?
> **SPRINGSTEEN:** No.

He'd answered my first question. But we arrived at the second question pretty damn fast. Fortunately, I had another one ready to go. But what of the first?

I wanted to see that room because something important was made there, and I wanted to know if by looking at a photograph of the space, I could see traces of what happened, the outlines of *Nebraska*. And maybe those photographic traces could bring it back to life for me, a resurrection. Photographs of his previous place, the Holmdel farmhouse, are easy to find online. Whether you see Springsteen in them or not, whether the amps and guitars are in the room or not, you look at them knowing who was there once and what got done at the time, *Darkness on the Edge of Town* and much of *The River*. The rooms begin to breathe.

Apparently even Bob Dylan had made his own attempt to see one of Springsteen's creative spaces, empty and well after the fact. There was a rainy night in Long Branch, New Jersey,

2009, when police picked up Dylan in a neighborhood close to where Springsteen wrote most if not all of the *Born to Run* album. Some quick if speculative reporting captured the incident.

The police had approached Dylan when the future Nobel Prize winner was on the grounds of a home up for sale, apparently investigating the property. The proximity to Springsteen's former rental, coupled with Dylan's somewhat recent visits to Neil Young's and John Lennon's childhood homes, gave interested journalists a basis from which to work. *The Guardian* reported it this way:

> Probing musicians' backgrounds who influenced the world of rock in the 1960s and 1970s is a hobby for Dylan. Last November he turned up unannounced at a Winnipeg house where the Canadian rock star Neil Young grew up. Kiernan and Patti Regan came home from shopping to find him waiting on their doorstep and invited him in.
>
> Then, in May, Dylan paid a £16 entrance fee and mingled anonymously with tourists at the childhood home of John Lennon in Woolton, Liverpool.
>
> Finally, last month, homeowners in Long Branch, 30 miles south of New York, phoned the authorities when they noticed a scruffy figure ambling along a residential street and entering the yard of an up-for-sale house.
>
> Soaking wet, Dylan, 68, gave his name to Kristie Buble, a 24-year-old police officer, and informed her that he was in town to headline a concert with country star Willie Nelson and rocker John Mellencamp. She was sceptical.

Dylan was, it seems, just behaving like, say, a Melville reader given the chance to peer into the modest Berkshires room where the author wrote *Moby-Dick,* or a Hitchcock fan presented with the opportunity to inspect the room where the director collaborated on *Vertigo*'s storyboards. Something vast that couldn't fit in such spaces came from them nonetheless. Surely that's worth a look.

Springsteen's Long Branch rental was, at some point in the 1970s, filled with characters, Jersey Shore dumps, confessions, lies, dreams, rusted-out cars, love—and Springsteen put it all in an order that he called *Born to Run.* You couldn't look in that rental and see all of that then, and you can't see it now. But we know it happened there, so we see differently, with our imaginations as much as our eyes.

Nebraska came from a bedroom in Colts Neck, another rental, this time a ranch house. My first question in the interview was just an attempt to go by the place, to look at it with Springsteen. The imagery of *Nebraska,* the electric chairs, the batons, the radio towers, the taillights, the people and their quiet desperation, they all passed through that room. But as Springsteen told me, no photographs exist. So I moved on to my second question: Why *Nebraska,* why right then? To which he replied,

It was a strange moment. I came off the *River* Tour and I
felt that hollowness. Part of it was just my time, I was
thirty-two, thirty-three. I was living literally five minutes
up the road from here. It was right before my first big
crash, my depressive crash, you know, that I had in 1982.

This was just before that, and there was a lot of strange stuff in the air. In my life, I guess.

In the absence of photographs, Springsteen gave me in words what I was going to need in order to get into that room. So that's how we spent the afternoon, driving by a place that was no longer there, that only he could see.

CHAPTER TWO

The Golden Age of Bands

So then I went over to Paul's and knocked on his door. I said the same thing: "I'm leaving the band. I feel you three guys are really close and I'm out of it." And Paul said, "I thought it was you three!"

—RINGO STARR, *The Beatles Anthology*

It used to be that students were expected to make their own book covers to protect school property textbooks. Brown paper bags, cut, fitted, and taped in place, often served such a purpose. The covers could be customized, scrawled with boyfriends' and girlfriends' names, Aerosmith lyrics, abstract patterns expressing a total lack of interest in classrooms, stickers from Wacky Packages, scribbled tirades. I remember when my brother decorated his math and history book covers with images of Bruce Springsteen, taken from the covers of *Time* and *Newsweek*. This happened in Concord, New Hampshire, fall 1975. At that time and in that place Bruce Springsteen was as foreign to my brother's classmates as was Bob Marley. That was going to change, in both cases, but my brother was out in front of things for the time being.

We watched as the Springsteen phenomenon grew, and grew, until Led Zeppelin no longer provided the soundtrack for parking lot activities outside the Concord High School football field. New Hampshire was a backwater, often among the last places to embrace whatever was coming next. From *The Wild, the Innocent & the E Street Shuffle* forward we were watching the artist's moves, waiting for the recordings, checking in at Pitchfork Records on Main Street, and getting the latest releases as soon as they were available. Every album seemed like a part of some meaningful progression. Springsteen was an index of where things were at and, more important, where they might be headed.

Once my brother and I were playing in the Del Fuegos, doing gigs in Boston, then New York, we'd meet other musicians who had watched Springsteen in the way we had. Scott Kempner was one of them. He'd been in the Dictators, then formed the Del-Lords. Our band would join the latter on a Folk City bill that also featured the New York City debut of the Replacements. There were several people there that night who had spent long hours listening to Bruce Springsteen records, looking at album jackets, thinking about "the factory girls underneath the boardwalk, where they all promise to unsnap their jeans."

There wasn't a lot of rock and roll on the charts that also mattered to musicians in early 1980s underground bands. Springsteen was an exception. He hadn't cut the cords that connected him to the bars and one-bedroom apartments we knew so well. So we all watched him as if he were one of us. Because Scott Kempner was a little older than we were, though, he was one musician on the Folk City bill who had a perspective on Springsteen that exceeded our own. He actually knew the guy. That was something.

When *Nebraska* came out, Kempner was telling everyone: you have to hear this record. He believed *Nebraska* was special. When Los Angeles's Blasters came into town for a gig, Dave Alvin, the group's songwriter and guitar player, slept on Scott Kempner's couch. This was how the system worked, if it could be called a system. "I was staying at Scott's, and it's all they were talking about, *Nebraska*," Alvin recalls. "So I picked it up once we got back home, and I understood."

There were bands across the country thinking about *Nebraska*, telling one another they had to listen. Springsteen was known as a bandleader, but this recording wasn't a band thing. So what did it mean? Since the time of the early Beatles, rock and roll groups were the locus of identity for many young American males. For those who went after it, to be in a band was to *be*. People struggled to get into them. I knew why, if only because I experienced it from the inside. When my brother brought me into the Del Fuegos, a lot of things made sense, and right away. I belonged. And when I quit, not talking to him for two years after some brutal exchanges? I didn't belong. You were in or you were out. I found that people were often less vocal about the patience and fortitude required to stay in a band. Bands could break your heart. Springsteen spoke plainly about this the day I visited, about how his own group managed to keep being a band, and over a period of decades.

"It took a lot of sorting out over the years," he told me. "There's a lot of displacement of emotion and enmeshment that occurs with your band that is not necessarily good for either the band or yourself. So, yeah, we've lasted a long time, amazingly enough, but there's been a psychological progression in the band itself that has allowed us to remain as connected as we are today. Otherwise we'd have broken up like most bands do."

But with *Nebraska,* Springsteen had figured out the crucial if counterintuitive truth: one of the ways to keep the band together, to stay connected, was to disconnect. *Nebraska* was an example of that in practice. "Bands break up 'cause they can't make that psychological progression," Springsteen went on to say. "They don't have the skills or ability. So if you're going to stay together, you have to make that progression, unless you're just doing it for economic reasons. We're one of the few bands who really made that leap of consciousness into another state of development that kept us creatively vital and also simply together. *Nebraska* defined that I was going to have a work life that involved working with the band and sometimes not working with the band. That was the first record that laid that out."

No one knew right then, in 1982, that the golden age of bands was like other golden ages, bound to end. There may always be pockets of band activity, new iterations driven by new technologies and new ripples from the margins, even movements, like grunge or indie rock. But the day of concert and club bills made up almost entirely of bands would come to a close. The late Adam Schlesinger of Fountains of Wayne described a period during which his band's 2003 hit, "Stacy's Mom," put them on some dates with other charting performers. No other act, he said, was lugging a drum kit and amps onto the stage. As a four-piece combo of two guitars, bass, and drums, they were a curiosity.

When Springsteen went from *The River* to *Nebraska,* he went from the world of the band into another experience, isolated. To some people who played in groups it looked like freedom, to others a concern, to some a front man's indulgence. If you'd put all your money down on that thing the Beatles and the Rolling Stones represented, this called for a moment of pause. A band guy left every trace of that tradition behind, then called it his best work.

———

Scott Kempner, like so many others in the mid-1960s, had figured out early that playing in a rock and roll band was the best thing on offer for a young man of limited means. You didn't have to read music. You didn't have to wake up early. Girls who otherwise wouldn't notice you might just show some interest. The American dream might not hold up under close inspection, but rock and roll offered an escape route and, sometimes, a hint of that dream. For a kid from the Bronx like Scott Kempner, born in 1954, the year of Elvis's first single on Sun Records, this was a way forward. You could leave home and have a different kind of family, bound by shared interests.

The Beatles and the Stones were only the most visible confirmations that playing in a rock and roll band was a line of work and a way of life with considerable upsides. And those were just the two biggest names; there were many, many more in that parade. Kempner was ten when the Beatles played on

The Ed Sullivan Show. By the time he was a teenager, he was seeing rock and roll bands everywhere. Why work in a bank?

Kempner was one among a legion of like-minded young people who heard that call. Young men, that is. However progressive the culture that emerged around rock and roll, when it came to gender, things were coded male. By 1966 there were so many kids wanting in on the band thing that music stores struggled to keep Ringo drum kits in stock. Of course, as Kempner and so many others would discover, there was one significant problem with bands: every one of them included other members.

Bruce Springsteen, five years older than Kempner, was another East Coast guy who started playing in groups without pausing to consider the alternatives. Later in his life, Springsteen would insist that this was so only because there *were* no alternatives. Both men would be in and out of groups throughout their lives, seemingly unable to stop, despite what they had learned along the way, despite the accumulation of disappointments and adjustments to the ideal.

"I remember when the first Bruce record came out, and he was the new Dylan," Kempner recalls. "Like right off the bat. I couldn't believe that anybody had the nerve to even use that. I understand that it was the record label, the promotion department that was responsible. But I thought, 'I don't need to ever hear this guy.' First reaction." Kempner was right that it wasn't Springsteen's idea. And Springsteen, who for years resisted the "new Dylan" tag and lived with it as a burden, not a blessing, was right in thinking that any promotional campaign sounding that "new Dylan" refrain risked alienating the very audience members who mattered the most. But in time the records would have their way with Kempner.

"A year or so after hearing all that 'new Dylan' stuff, the Dictators were standing outside this recording studio," Kempner recalls. "It's like midnight, before we all go our separate ways, and Andy [Shernoff] goes, 'You know, I heard this new Springsteen album, the follow-up.' I figure he's gonna tell me it was a piece of shit. He says, 'I think you better hear it.' I said, 'Why?'"

Andy Shernoff didn't elaborate, just told Kempner he should check it out. The Dictators and Springsteen were label mates at Columbia, so Kempner could get a free promo copy of *The Wild, the Innocent & the E Street Shuffle*. He went up to Columbia the next day. "I asked for a copy from the label," Kempner says, "and I think it was all I listened to for like six months, maybe more. I couldn't believe that record. I didn't want to hear anything else."

At that time, the Dictators were managed and produced by Murray Krugman and Sandy Pearlman, the team that handled Blue Öyster Cult. This meant that, among other things, Scott Kempner could get on the guest list when Blue Öyster Cult shared the bill with Rod Stewart and the Faces at Madison Square Garden. That was on February 24, 1975. The Faces, widely considered one of the great rock and roll bands, were struggling in the shadows of their lead singer's solo career. Stewart's "Maggie May" alone eclipsed anything the Faces would ever release. The Faces' next U.S. tour would be their last, while that singer, Rod Stewart, would have several more costume changes coming. His disco hit "Da Ya Think I'm Sexy?" was just three years off.

Backstage at the Garden for the Blue Öyster Cult/Faces show was a lavish affair. In Kempner's words it was "a tons-of-food thing." One Faces crew member described the group's touring style as being "like the good old days of the Wild West in America, when Jesse James and his men would ride into town, take all the money, have all the women, and ride into the next town and do the same thing. It was like a hurricane passing through. Everyone had a drink in their hand around the clock." It also meant that catering was at times exceptional. Kempner got to the Garden and went straight for the buffet, and then it was only a matter of finding a spot at a backstage table where no one would bother him while he ate.

"I'm walking around, very few seats, most of the tables have like maybe one spot left," Kempner recalled. "Finally, I get to this table, and there's this one guy eating there at the end with a few empty seats around him. I walk over there, and before I could say anything I realize it's fucking Bruce Springsteen." Free food was free food, and neither of these Columbia artists had much in their refrigerators back home. Getting signed to a major label like Columbia didn't really mean a lot until you had hits, and even then it could be years before an artist experienced the material rewards associated with success. In the meantime, you got what you could of Rod Stewart's duck pâté.

"I walk up," Kempner continued, "and say, 'Bruce, I just wanted to tell you I've been listening to your record since I got it like months ago.' He smiles, thanks me. I say, 'We're label mates. I'm in the Dictators.' And then he stood straight up, like bolted to his feet, and said, 'You're in the *Dictators*? I saw you guys. Stevie took me to the Bottom Line. I couldn't believe it,

I wanted to meet you, but I was too nervous.' I was all of a sudden in the twilight zone." Springsteen told Kempner to sit down, and the two guys in bands talked for an hour, mostly about bands.

They'd meet again within the year, when Kempner was sitting in the booth of the Carnegie Hall Cinema, where his girlfriend was tearing tickets. When he didn't have a gig, Kempner would keep her company. After she finished work, they'd take a bus back to the Bronx. It was winter and one of New York City's coldest nights. Kempner and his girlfriend had a space heater in the ticket booth. It was a double feature of *Mean Streets* and *The Wild Bunch*. Kempner was looking at the people in the line when he saw Springsteen, wearing only a leather jacket and backward baseball hat. He knew that Springsteen, despite having *Born to Run* in the stores by that time, would probably be grateful if Kempner's girlfriend could comp a ticket, save him the five bucks. He was right.

A few years after *that,* the Dictators were in the recording studio next to the E Street Band at the Record Plant, and by then the two groups had a kinship. The E Street Band was working on *Darkness on the Edge of Town,* the Dictators on *Bloodbrothers.* "They came a few days after us," Kempner recalled. "Months later they were still there, and we were long gone. But there were only two rooms on the ground floor, and then there was the lounge to share. So for the two months we *were* there, we all saw each other every single day." As is often the case, more happened in the lounge than in the studios.

"We got to know everyone in the band," Kempner explained, "especially Bruce and Clarence, which was the real revelation of the whole deal. Their relationship was so obviously special and apart from everything else, except maybe Bruce's with Stevie. But Bruce and Clarence, the two of them could do any *Honeymooners* top to bottom. They just had this thing. It radiated from the two of them. Clarence would sneak into our studio with us 'cause we were potheads. He would come in the studio and smoke with us. Then he'd always go, 'You guys aren't gonna tell the Boss, right?' We were like, 'Clarence, we're not the kind of guys who tell anything on anybody ever. You can be sure we're not gonna tell Bruce you're smoking pot with us.'"

The main reason the members of the E Street Band and the members of the Dictators understood one another, however, wasn't that every one of them had some experience of street life, whether on one side of the Hudson or the other. Yes, the street gave them a common language, but what really bound them was the fact that they'd all spent their entire adult lives playing in rock and roll bands. Shifting, defining, rich in misunderstanding, glorious, sick with hidden aspirations, delicate beyond comprehension: bands were the mystery they all called home.

"One of the first days we were recording *Bloodbrothers,* Bruce comes back from lunch with what looks like a poster in a poster tube," Kempner recalled. "He's got a hammer. He's got one of those little clear boxes of different nails. He comes into our recording studio, takes out this poster—it's the poster of Brigitte Bardot on the motorcycle—hammers it into the wall, and looks at it like he's so proud of himself. Like he figures this has *gotta be* so up their alley, these Dictator guys. And of course it was. We were a rock and roll band."

During those Springsteen sessions at the Record Plant, preparing to record the song "Darkness on the Edge of Town," the E Street Band set up in a room that was in the process of being rebuilt. It was bare concrete walls, unfinished and not intended for recording, exactly the kind of room you were supposed to avoid when making records. It was alive to a fault, and Springsteen loved it. You couldn't mistake the sound they got for anything other than a band playing together.

For Springsteen's next record, *The River,* he'd go even deeper into that band thing. If *Born to Run* was a record that sounded like a record, like a production, *The River,* recorded at Manhattan's Power Station, would be the record that sounded like a band, hammering away in a room, sounds ricocheting off the walls. It was an effort to capture *and convey* the idea that guys like Springsteen and Kempner had given their lives to: the rock and roll band.

Until it stops working, to be in a band was to have an instant identity, a badge and license. The proof of belonging was those other members. And when everyone was in on it, committed and sworn in, staring down the same ambitions, nothing and no one could fuck with that. That's how it felt on the inside. That's what Springsteen was after with *The River,* to capture the sound inside that experience, as it happened on a stage. And he did it the way he'd always done it, obsessively.

CHAPTER THREE

The Sound Inside That Thing

[With *Nebraska*] I was writing a type of song that I probably would have been embarrassed to sit down and sing in front of the band in the studio. If I could have sung it at all, it wouldn't have been the same. If I'd gone in the studio and just introduced that music in a normal way, I don't know if *Nebraska* would ever have occurred.

—BRUCE SPRINGSTEEN, in conversation with the author, 2021

You can't get to *Nebraska* without going back to *The River*. Because *Nebraska* was born somewhere in all that noise. *Nebraska* would signal changes that Springsteen would call "the end of something." And that would include the first part of his life as the leader of the E Street Band.

As a recording, *The River* was a confrontation contained on four sides of a double album. "I wanted to cut some music," Springsteen said, "that felt very explosive." As a record, it careened and contradicted itself. It was something of a wreck, and in being a wreck restored a crucial understanding that the message and meaning of rock and roll didn't always get clearer when a recording's fidelity and organization did. *The River* implicitly argued that imperfection is the essential ingredient of rock and roll performance.

But setting out to capture the sound of a *band,* a loud version of the Truth that had originally promised to set young men like Bruce Springsteen and Scott Kempner free, Springsteen faced the thing itself in the earliest hours of work. No sooner than the end of the first day of recording *The River,* Steven Van Zandt told Springsteen he was quitting. The guitar player said he couldn't go through that E Street Band experience in the studio one more time.

Van Zandt was referring to what happened with *Darkness on the Edge of Town,* the many months of struggle involved in finding the record Springsteen had in his mind, a process that might have been easier, of course, if Springsteen's mind didn't keep changing. *Darkness on the Edge of Town* had been a fight, and the first day of recording its follow-up seemed to Van Zandt a sure sign that some repetition compulsion was at work in the psyche of Bruce Springsteen.

As Van Zandt recalled to Springsteen's biographer Peter Ames Carlin, he took Springsteen aside and made his position clear. "I said, 'Listen, I'm sorry but I can't do this again. You carry on, but I quit. I'm splitting.'" In Van Zandt's recollection, Springsteen quickly promised it would be different. Which makes sense, because you need a band to capture the sound of a band. And even if one of the most common sounds a band makes is "I quit," it's not a sound that can fill an album. Springsteen needed his bandmate for noises other than that. Carlin writes,

Van Zandt was having none of it. The real problem, he told Bruce, was that his production team—he, Landau, and the rest of their production team—"didn't have a fucking idea about what they're doing." Speaking thirty-one years later, he reins in his critique of everyone except Bruce and his pathological work habits. "They all had their talents, I knew that. But contemplating the whole fucking years it was gonna take to make a record, I couldn't do that. Didn't have the patience. And that's when he said, 'No, no, I want you to produce it with me.' And that's a direct quote."

Van Zandt was willing to stay under those new conditions. Which meant that contrary to what he told Springsteen, he *could* do it again, if he got a producer credit. It wasn't exactly a job interview that landed him the position. It was Van Zandt, as a key band member, threatening to leave, and a bandleader managing that situation in the most expedient fashion. It's hard to imagine that Springsteen had that warm, all-for-one-and-one-for-all feeling at the end of that particular business day. But at least he knew everyone would show up for work the next afternoon.

So, starting from day two of recording *The River*, there were three producers on the project, Bruce Springsteen, Jon Landau, and Steven Van Zandt. And, really, the negotiation that landed Van Zandt his producer credit *would* help get Springsteen what he wanted: a band record with a band sound. But Van Zandt was right. It was going to take an unreasonably long amount of time. Van Zandt would quit again, midway through recording *Born in the U.S.A.* And he'd join again, after what he would later describe to *Rolling Stone* as seven years of walking his dog.

Of course, by the time the dog walking was done, with Van

Zandt back in the group, the E Street Band wasn't the same thing it had been in 1979. It's a law of rock and roll bands that each "negotiation" along the lines of Van Zandt's at the beginning of The River sessions erodes the ideal form that once signaled freedom for all. The struggle and erosion are intrinsic to a band's life. The miracle is that, in the case of the E Street Band, there still is a band.

———————

Though Springsteen's recording career started as one man's contract with Columbia Records and would remain one man's contract, he was still raised under the sign of the Beatles. The being-in-a-band mattered deeply, from the beginning. To Springsteen as to Van Zandt. In 1979, 1980, neither was done with it. Not yet. And, yes, The River would be the high point in trying to make a group sound central to the work of a man under contract as a solo artist. The mission was, on many levels, a shared mission. As a project, The River had purpose, intention, and a target. Mostly.

When the album was finally done, its artwork would underscore the sound of the recordings with a visual message. There are photographs of a group, playing together, recording at the Power Station, in rehearsals, on a park bench, on a rooftop, in the street. You saw more of that band in The River artwork than in any other Springsteen album design before or after.

The bandleader, at times looking like Gene Vincent, was alone only on the cover of The River. The fans who bought and held the album, staring into its images to unearth its secrets, saw a guy in a band, surrounded. When they dropped the needle, they mostly heard the same thing coming from the speakers. And there was no mistaking *where* it was all coming from. There were no palm trees in the photographs. It was East Coast rock and roll. You got the sense that even if all the inner sleeve photographs *had* been in color, they still would have been black and white. In that place, the asphalt, the leather jackets, and the trees were all the same color.

With the sounds bleeding together, *The River* felt like an embodied argument against an earlier, mid-1960s shift in emphasis that had affected most if not all of popular music. Since the Beatles' *Sgt. Pepper's* and the Beach Boys' *Pet Sounds,* recording studio work had been made a kind of priority, with live performance often assuming a supporting role. When Brian Wilson stopped performing with the Beach Boys, focusing instead on the group's majestic recordings, or when the Beatles came off the road permanently in 1966 to focus on the studio, they made a point about what mattered.

Records. The recording studio. Performances? They were typically meant to represent and promote the latest album. It wasn't the way James Brown thought about things. Brown had his mind on the show and made records along the way. Springsteen was out to restore some balance. So *The River* reversed the priorities; it was a project meant to capture in the studio what happened on the stage, rather than vice versa. He wanted to make a record that could give listeners a taste of what happened up there during a live show, when everyone in the band responded to the same *one, two, three, four!*

West Coast acts like the Eagles, Fleetwood Mac, and Linda Ronstadt had dominated the mid-1970s with crisp and controlled recordings, gorgeous stuff. They labored, they layered, they separated musicians into different studio spaces to avoid bleed in the microphones. Onstage those same acts attempted to realize in the live setting what they'd done in the studio. And if they had to stand stock-still to do it, they would. It wasn't like an R&B revue at the Apollo. That's not to suggest that great albums didn't come of it all. Ronstadt's *Heart Like a Wheel* is just one example of the often stunning results. But for some, the teachings of early rock and roll had been lost and the pendulum needed to swing back in the other direction.

The River would ride on top of that pendulum as if it were one part roller coaster, one part wrecking ball. Something needed tearing down, and the destruction, Springsteen believed, could be a thrill ride. The No Nukes concert of 1979, held in the middle of *The River* sessions, put Springsteen and the E Street Band up against the mellow self-presentation of Crosby, Stills & Nash, Jackson Browne, the Doobie Brothers, James Taylor, and others. There, too, a point was going to be made: you don't need to sacrifice the physicality and performativity of a real rock and roll show to deliver the emotion associated with the singer-songwriter's solo trip—you could do both and kill the place.

Even Tom Petty and the Heartbreakers, representing a California very different from that of the other acts at No Nukes, had to contend with the sheer force of Springsteen's show. The arena belonged to Springsteen for both of their two nights. When Petty was getting ready to take the stage in the slot before the E Street Band, a member of the stage crew urged him to make no mistakes regarding that sound coming from the audience: "Don't worry, they're not booing. They're saying, 'Bruce.'" Petty looked at him, quietly replying, "Which is worse?" Then he took the stage.

Nick Hornby, writing for *The Guardian* years later, weighed it all, thinking of Springsteen's reworking of the James Brown "cape routine" and self-conscious drive to have a show on the Madison Square Garden stage. "What's remarkable, looking at it now," Hornby writes, "is that Springsteen's uncomplicated showbiz gestures seem way more 'authentic' than all the smiley, gleaming-teeth sincerity that James Taylor, Carly Simon and the rest of the performers are trying to project. What, after all, could be more sincere than a performer performing—and acknowledging that he's performing." No Nukes was a kind of midcourse confirmation that the direction *The River* was taking—"let's get this show on record"—was indeed the right one. The Madison Square Garden audiences had cast their vote.

After the No Nukes performances and back at the Power Station, continuing work on *The River,* Springsteen was ever more committed to capturing on record that energy of an ensemble born to the club circuit, just as he was determined to keep some rock and roll in the arenas. Contrasting his ambitions as a record maker to those of the Southern California school and what he called its "almost stultifying attention to detail," Springsteen spells out his ambitions in *Born to Run:*

> We wanted open room mikes, smashing drums (the snare sound on Elvis's "Hound Dog" was my Holy Grail), crashing cymbals, instruments bleeding into one another and a

voice sounding like it was fighting out from the middle of a brawling house party. We wanted the sound of *less* control. This was how many of our favorite records from the early days of rock 'n' roll had been recorded. You miked the band *and* the room. You *heard* the band and the room. The sonic characteristics of the room were essential in the quality and personality of your recording. The room brought the messiness, the realness, the can't-get-out-of-each-other's-way togetherness of musicians in search of "that sound."

He described it all in the name of "we," the rock and roll band pronoun of choice. The *can't-get-out-of-each-other's-way* pronoun. *That* "we."

But as a record out to capture the glory of what happened onstage with the E Street Band, *The River*'s conceptual framing didn't serve all its material equally well. In his own writing, Springsteen would say that one hope he had in making the record was to leaven the "unrelenting seriousness" of *Darkness on the Edge of Town* with something lighter that happened in front of an audience. This, it seems, was an ambition Van Zandt could help him realize. "With Steve's encouragement," Springsteen writes, "I began to steer the record into a rawer direction. This is the album where the E Street Band hit its stride." To Peter Ames Carlin, Springsteen would say that he "wanted to combine the fun aspect of what the band did along with the story I was telling." The question would be whether listeners went to *recordings* looking for the same things they got from live shows. Did the fun matter in the same way in both situations?

Just a few years after its release, Springsteen would speak of *The River* as an album that pulled in different directions, sharing his own thoughts on what others saw as its exuberant but undecided quality. "On *The River*," he told *Hot Press*, "I'd have a song like this and a song like that because I didn't know how to combine it." After first delivering the album to Columbia as a single LP titled *The Ties That Bind*, Springsteen put a stop to the release. Something was troubling him already. In conversation with Robert Hilburn, when the double album was finally in stores, he explained, "I had an album of 13 songs finished a year ago September, but I didn't put the record out because it wasn't personal enough. This album seems much more personal to me."

"Personal." Not a band word, a songwriter word, a Springsteen word. And the "personal" was the thing in jeopardy when the can't-get-out-of-each-other's-way aspect was emphasized. It's hard to get both those elements on the same recording. Springsteen had managed it before, but that didn't mean it was a simple matter. One writer, trying to describe the ultimate form *The River* assumed, pegged it as "less Kierkegaard, lots more Kingsmen and Bobby Fuller Four."

Maybe *The River* still "wasn't personal enough," even after the balance was addressed. The spectrum of the album's material was wide, with a song like "Crush on You" at one end and something along the lines of "Stolen Car" at the other. "Crush on You" has all the immediacy of a song written moments before it was recorded, and you can hear the band having a hell of a good time putting it down, Springsteen screaming his way through a lyric that you don't need to know to understand. But no one was going to corner Springsteen and tell him that "Crush on You" told the story of their life. "Stolen Car," quite differently, felt like a poet at work. You hear every word. The production is skeletal, built around Springsteen's strummed electric guitar and Roy Bittan's piano. Distant background vocals and drums enter partway through but remain at a distance. An organ gets its place, but only when Springsteen's vocal is complete.

While songs as different as "Crush on You" and "Stolen Car" could coexist in a live show, helping to establish the rhythm of a performance, they couldn't always do that on record. Not easily, at least. Records and live shows are indeed two different mediums, no matter the Venn diagram overlap. Springsteen would later describe "Crush on You" as the "worst song we ever put on record." But about "Stolen Car" he felt differently. "A song like this and a song like that." And, really, it was the beginning of bigger differences between the bandleader and his guitar player and co-producer. A producer like this and a producer like that.

In contrast to the more meditative, story-driven existentialism of "Stolen Car," "Crush on You" wasn't pulled from the inner life of a songwriter. It was the kind of song that happened when a band turned up the Fender amplifiers, paid little mind to the neighbors, and ignored the landlord's calls. It wasn't about introspection. It didn't stare into any abyss, walk into any solitude. But it was probably a great feeling to play it as a combo. "Stolen Car," on the other hand, was the sound of a man who told stories even when he was in a room by himself, a lost one singing of lost ones. That storyteller, because he was making a particular kind of band record, brought in his group to support even the "Stolen Car" kinds of tales. If there was a schizophrenic quality to *The River* that was in some way essential to its character, it had to do with the swing between these two types of songs. No such swing would animate *The River*'s follow-up. It would be Springsteen going in one direction without looking back, leaving everyone and everything behind. "The end of something."

"It's this stuff that he completely ignores about himself that is, to me, his highest evolution," Steven Van Zandt would later remark. "It's easy to be personal. It's easy to be original, believe it or not. Pink Floyd is easy. 'Louie Louie' is hard." Springsteen's old friend was operating with a significantly different value system, challenging the importance of the very thing at which Springsteen excelled, the personal, while also believing that he, perhaps better than anyone, understood the songwriter Bruce Springsteen. "I knew exactly what he sounded like," Van Zandt would say, "exactly what the band sounded like, exactly what he heard in his head, and how he needed the next album to sound." Springsteen, a man who asked questions, had a co-producer who specialized in answers. On the best days it worked out in a yin-yang kind of fashion. And then there were the other days.

As herd animals, band members do their best work when they can think with one mind, when their shared interests bring them together in some clumsy yet glorious movement forward. "Look, there's water over there. Let's go get some." But when one of them wanders off by himself, looking for a thing the others *don't* have in mind . . . it's a different experience of the prairie. Gone is the oneness. The *River* Tour was going to be an unforgettable message about what a rock and roll band could be and could do. The energy of live performance that Springsteen captured with that recording he would bring to the legendary tour that followed. Both were not just great successes, they were lasting statements about rock and roll. But the "Stolen Car" part of Springsteen, that personal part, was the heartbeat beneath the floorboards.

For some, the "personal" approach to songwriting might seem like a choice to be made, almost a stylistic decision. For Springsteen it would never be that. It's just who he is. "I'm an alienated person by nature," Springsteen told Brian Hiatt in 2010. "Always have been, still am to this day. It continues to be an issue in my life, in that I'm always coming from the outside, and I'm always trying to overcome my own internal reticence and alienation. Which is funny, because I throw myself the opposite way onstage, but the reason I do that is because while the stage and all those people are out there, the abyss is under my heels, and I always feel it back there." *The River* was only partially about the "back there." *Nebraska* would balance things out. It was all back there.

CHAPTER FOUR

Suicide in the Hallways

Even my melody is reduced to next to nothing on *Nebraska*. Melody would have ruined it totally. It just wasn't austere enough. The austerity was much more important.

—BRUCE SPRINGSTEEN, in conversation with the author, 2021

The Power Station, where *The River* was recorded, is located in a former Con Edison power transfer building on Manhattan's West Fifty-Third Street. In 1979 the neighborhood was still dirty, on the outskirts of Broadway and close enough to Times Square to get a whiff of the booze on its breath. New York wasn't yet cleaned up for tourist traffic. After Con Edison moved out, but before Chic and the Rolling Stones would cut records there, the building was used as a soundstage for Monty Hall's *Let's Make a Deal* and television's gothic soap opera *Dark Shadows.* That weirdness was no doubt part of the studio's aura.

The music chapter in the building's history began in 1977 when Tony Bongiovi redesigned the site for recording. Bongiovi had some innate gift for sound. When just a teen in Raritan, New Jersey, he cold-called Motown Records. In the course of that phone conversation, someone at Motown picked up on Bongiovi's strengths and flew him to Detroit to work at their studio. Tony was that kind of kid. After opening the Power Station, he let his second cousin sweep the place in exchange for studio time. The demos that second cousin made led to the signing of a group called Bon Jovi and, as it happened, years of lawsuits between the relatives. That's another New Jersey story.

When the E Street Band set up camp at the Power Station to cut *The River,* Springsteen often stayed at a New York hotel facing the southern side of Central Park. It was as close to being on the road as he could be without changing cities each night. The walk from the hotel to the studio was short, but Springsteen would, in the end, know it in every season. True to Steven Van Zandt's forecast on day one of the sessions, the making of *The River* went far longer than was projected. After delivering that single album, *The Ties That Bind,* to his label and then taking it back almost as quickly, Springsteen wrote more and more songs, eventually spending his own money to record them, until there wasn't a whole lot of money left. They were at the Power Station for well over a year.

During that time, as both the pleasure and the point of the work became less obvious, it was much as it had been back at the Record Plant, with other acts working down the hall, on another floor, passing through the lounge, waiting for the bathroom. However insular the big recording studios were, cut off from life outside, like gated communities of creative striving and sloth (in equal measures), inside they allowed contact with the other artists who were coming and going. Very few acts stayed as long as the E Street Band, but those who booked time in that period often met Springsteen and his band, all of whom were increasingly interested in people who were not in the E Street Band.

Carly Simon and Diana Ross were both working at the Power Station in that period, the latter making a record with Nile Rodgers and Bernard Edwards of Chic. Ric Ocasek of the Cars was there producing Suicide. If you wanted to mark a point that's as far from the Eagles' *Hotel California* as you can get, Alan Vega and Martin Rev's Suicide might be it. Oddly enough, for the recording of their debut, Suicide had used the less illustrious 914 Studios in Blauvelt, New York, where *Born to Run* was recorded. But *that* shared experience hadn't led to any interactions between Alan Vega and Bruce Springsteen.

The Power Station would be the place where the two men would get to know each other. It was an odd but lasting connection that would mean less to *The River* than it would to *Nebraska*. Of *Nebraska,* one critic would go so far as to say that without Suicide "we wouldn't have *Nebraska*." Carly Simon had a different experience of Suicide. In Alan Vega's recollection, Carly Simon responded to Suicide with a "disgusted look," which was more in line with what the duo was accustomed to.

By most accounts, Suicide didn't make it easy to be a fan, so they didn't collect them with great regularity. The name alone had a come-no-further quality. But time and a few influential believers have done their part to bestow "historical significance" on Suicide, some of those believers identifying in the group an early ancestor of the electronic music that would later rise to dominance. By the twenty-first century, somewhere out in Bushwick, it was a little cooler to say you were into Suicide. Of course, that's not when Bruce Springsteen got interested in the group, or where, or why.

Suicide called themselves "punk" as early as 1970, a year after Woodstock and somewhere around Johnny Rotten's fourteenth birthday, well before the term's usage soared. The word was printed in their flyers. But come 1976 and 1977, when punk emerged as a phenomenon, Suicide didn't look like punk, if only because they lacked some of the genre's defining features, such as a drummer and a guitar player. They weren't like the Ramones or the Clash, Elvis Costello and the Attractions or Blondie. There was a classification dilemma, based in part on all that was missing. It was two men, one doing things with a microphone, the other playing electronic instruments, early synthesizers and drum machines, among other things.

No matter that Suicide was on bills with the Ramones and every other act among those mentioned above, they would need every kindness history had to offer before they were welcomed into the punk category or seen as "fathers" of electronic music. They shared stages not just with those referenced but also with the New York Dolls, Richard Hell, Talking Heads, and others. But not infrequently, they were asked to get off those stages. Alan Vega described having to block a door to keep people *in* the room during a performance.

Rolling Stone's review of Suicide's debut called it "puerile." *The Village Voice* described it as "meaningless," "a con." Even at the time of Vega's death in 2016, the *New York Times* obituary, written by Jon Pareles, referred to Suicide as being "as much a provocation as a concert act." More telling, Pareles remarked that Suicide's music would "later be more widely tolerated." Tolerated? Not the word you'd expect in a musician's *New York Times* obituary. A YouTube clip captures a moment during a Suicide opening set when an arena full of Cars fans got its act together enough to shout in unison, "Fuck you! Fuck you! Fuck you!"

All of which meant that Bruce Springsteen, after meeting Alan Vega in the Power Station's hallways, was sometimes traveling in a pack of one when singing Suicide's praises:

> "We first met Springsteen in 1980," remembers Vega [in the *New York Post*]. "He was recording *The River* and we were recording our second album in New York. I spent five or six days hanging out with him and driving around. Then we had a playback meeting for our album. There were three or four big shots from our label, and Bruce was there, too. After we played the album, there was deathly silence . . . except for Bruce, who said, 'That was f—king great.'"

"Suicide," Springsteen told me, "there was something in it that called to me. This very dangerous music that spoke to some part of you that music didn't always get to. It was quite influential on *Nebraska,* just the tone of it I would say. There was an unforgivingness in it that appealed to me and that I wanted as part of my own music." Vega looked to the 1950s, to early rock and roll, as an inspiration. But Suicide was anything but a nostalgia act.

"Early Elvis, Little Richard, Johnny Cash," Vega told one interviewer, trying to explain what music mattered to him most. "They represented that lonely man on the lonely street in the middle of a lonely nowhere. They're singing. They're doing their thing. It's a loner thing." Unlike many of the critics who reviewed Suicide over the years, Springsteen detected this thread of influence in the music. "I've liked Suicide for a long time," he told *Mojo*. "If Elvis came back from the dead, I think he would sound like Alan Vega."

Among the Suicide recordings that Bruce Springsteen would reference over the years is "Frankie Teardrop." In a 1984 *Rolling Stone* interview with Kurt Loder, Springsteen described it as "one of the most amazing records I think I ever heard." One critic describes that same recording as a "10-minute horror drone."

As it opens, "Frankie Teardrop" recalls a scene with which Springsteen himself is associated, that of a young, working-class man arriving home from a factory job to wife and baby. But from there it devolves into something much darker: murder, infanticide. Alan Vega's screams, signifying the baby's death by shooting, are about as troubling as anything you'll hear on record. The recording was the centerpiece of Suicide's 1977 debut. The "unforgiving" aspect was, of course, in both the recording's sound and the story told. If Vega was inspired by the 1950s, it was a 1950s of madness, of violence, a shadow world that lay far, far from Pat Boone's house.

As clearly as anything else, Springsteen's connection with Vega during the recording of *The River* marks the beginning of *Nebraska*'s emergence. Off-putting to many, Suicide was a powerful example of recorded music's widest possibilities. "Yeah, I guess Alan Vega was more of a performance artist than a singer-songwriter," Springsteen told me. "And we shared that interest in early rock and roll. The '60s is a whole different ball of wax. The fundamental nature of the roots of where I come from is pre-'60s. The E Street Band itself. After '64, we're not that influenced by psychedelia and all that kind of music. We're kind of rooted in blue-collar, 1950s aesthetic. I was always sort of just a circumstantial hippie; the few years that I lived that lifestyle, it was just, I got thrust into it. By life. But I connected with Alan on a musical level, among other things."

Suicide's recordings whispered in Springsteen's ear, telling him there was a world of music, much of it unmapped, that extended well beyond the realm of the songs that often decided popular music's character. Love, celebration, romance in all its vicissitudes, these were popular music's common themes, and much of it was wrapped in a melodic allure and danceable rhythms. Suicide said that music had some other places it could go.

As Springsteen labored to finish *The River,* reconceptualized as a double album, Suicide got his interest. They weren't a band, not really. They were a collaboration, a duo, closer to art rock than to rock and roll. They didn't sound like any of the references Springsteen had thrown out over the years. But they stuck with Springsteen, like a thing growing inside him as he tended to other business.

When it got to the point at which Springsteen had some eighty songs recorded for *The River,* he had to learn, again, how to stop. Finishing, that would remain Springsteen's challenge over the years. He could always write more, change the sequence, switch songs out, redo the artwork. To complete an album is to choose an arbitrary point at which to stop working, nothing more, and Springsteen didn't like making that choice, because, after that, you didn't have any choices.

They finally took the master tapes out to Chuck Plotkin's Clover Studios in L.A. to mix the double album. As Springsteen says of the moment they got there (caps all his): "WE DID NOT KNOW HOW TO MIX WHAT WE'D RECORDED!" Jimmy Iovine came by the studio with Tom Petty, as a friend and a trusted insider. Iovine worked both as a second engineer and as an engineer on earlier Springsteen projects but was now a producer working with Petty, Stevie Nicks, Bob Seger, and others. Iovine listened to what they'd done and couldn't find a better way to question what he felt were *The River*'s confused musical priorities than to ask, in his own wry fashion, when they were going to record the lead vocals. For his part, and in a style different from Iovine's, Petty told Bruce that he wanted to know what the words were, that he was invested. Some would say that when you can't understand what the singer's saying on a Bruce Springsteen record, you may want to rethink your mix.

But they would finish the album, with angst and doubt walking beside Springsteen the whole way. The record would come out on October 17, 1980, fourteen days after the start of a tour that would extend almost a year. Within less than a month after its release, *The River* was Springsteen's first number one album. By November 15, "Hungry Heart" was at number five on the Hot 100, his first top ten single. It was Springsteen's most broad-based success to date. The tour would be remembered as one of the E Street Band's greatest and as the tour that cracked Europe.

The *River* Tour was more than just a career high point, though. It was also the experience that found Springsteen exploring more deeply his unique standing as a public figure. So many earlier experiences of success, such as that of finding himself on the covers of *Time* and *Newsweek* simultaneously, were like things that happened to him. The best he could do in those situations was react. He downplayed the hype, ran from it, cursed it. But the success that came with *The River* was his own doing, something he himself shaped. Rather than react to it, he began thinking, more and more, what he could do with it.

Bruce Springsteen never studied a music industry how-to book in order to cultivate the E Street culture that grew up around him. His inner circle of bandmates and collaborators was the result of an almost natural growth, guided by Springsteen's instinct. No one really trained for the jobs they were doing. The manager, Jon Landau, was a writer and critic who became a producer. Then he found himself acting as Springsteen's manager, in part because no one else was doing the job, but also because it seemed as if he and Springsteen could have the necessary conversations that would foster Springsteen's growth. The E Street Band was a club act that learned how to be a recording band. This was how Springsteen wanted it. Describing the team he built up around himself, Springsteen explained his reasoning to me:

I was not interested in professionals. They like schedules. They like somebody who's going to approach their work as a piece of work, and not very obsessively. I was into crafting an *identity* that was very, very personal to me as a man. As an artist. That was the job that I was doing and needed to do. For myself, for my own inner life. So I needed people who innately understood that that was what we were crafting. I wanted to connect that identity with the very big picture of the country at large. And so, I had big ideas, and I had no problem spending all my time trying to bring them to fruition. So I needed people who were going to be willing to go in as deep as I needed and was willing to go myself. Generally those are not professionals, just people who were passionate and had some skills.

As an approach, Springsteen's is counterintuitive. Expertise, experience, a track record: these are the things artists are encouraged to look for when assembling a team. Not Springsteen. He went on:

Jon had managerial skills, and he could learn to be a manager. Charlie [Plotkin] had enough skills to mix *Darkness on the Edge of Town*. As far as I know, I'm not sure if he mixed any other records in his life, but he mixed that one quite well. But I've done that with a lot of people over the years—said, "Hey, man, just plug it in, and if it sounds okay coming back, we're good." These are people who are not carrying around any ideas about the way something must be made. They're about process. They're not invested in a *particular* process. I needed people who were not invested in that way. I knew this intuitively. 'Cause I was just a kid when Jon came on. I was my son's age. I was just flying by the seat of my pants.

Jon Landau knows the ship he came in on. "Me, Chuck, some others among us, we started doing things that we didn't normally do," he told me. "I didn't want to be a manager. I wanted to be like Holland–Dozier–Holland. I liked the art. The managers were the bad guys." Your résumé wasn't going to dictate the job in Bruce Springsteen's world. Springsteen got himself a manager who wasn't a manager, and together they went on a voyage of discovery.

Springsteen once described Landau as "the Clark to my Lewis." Two men bound in exploration, Lewis/Springsteen the captain, Clark/Landau his chosen co-leader. Thomas Jefferson gave Meriwether Lewis the gig leading the Corps of Discovery, and Lewis approached William Clark. Some fifty men joined them on their journey to explore the West, many getting venereal disease along the way. Maybe Springsteen's analogy is even better than at first it seemed.

But it all meant that the exploration would continue, because it was in the nature of what Springsteen had put together. Roles could shift, key players could suddenly do something they hadn't trained for. A roadie could engineer. And what applied to the others also applied to Springsteen. He would shift positions, consider what else he could be, keep digging to find what was down there.

CHAPTER FIVE

Following the River

Odysseus has become a stranger in his own land.

—DANIEL MENDELSOHN, *An Odyssey*

Perhaps the coincidence of the *River* Tour's earliest dates and Ronald Reagan's November 4, 1980, electoral win demanded from Springsteen some kind of conscious reconsideration of what he should be and do as a public figure himself. The day after Reagan's win, from a stage in Arizona, Springsteen said it plainly: "I don't know what you guys think about what happened last night, but I think it's pretty frightening."

Reagan, on the campaign trail just months before that victory, was asked if an actor could be president. Without hesitation, he replied, "How can a president *not* be an actor?" The 1980s were going to be a time of color and costume, of theater and pageant. The recession of the early 1980s was, of course, the gray and unmoving world that was reality for most Americans, the place out behind the showy sets that Reagan erected in his charismatic visioning exercises. Springsteen was thinking, more and more openly, about who he was in relation to all that. Another actor?

Then, a month or so after Reagan's electoral victory and some two months into the *River* Tour, on December 8, Mark David Chapman shot John Lennon outside New York City's Dakota building, where Lennon lived. The world needed more than a rock and roll party, and Springsteen knew it. "Crush on You" could provide an escape. But the question became one of whether escape alone was what that moment was calling for. What else could music do?

From the stage and in the interviews conducted during the tour, Springsteen spoke more and more of what he was thinking about, what he was reading. He talked about Joe Klein's Woody Guthrie biography, Howard Zinn's *A People's History of the United States,* a book called *The Pocket History of the United States.* Picking up a copy of Ron Kovic's *Born on the Fourth of July* between tour dates, he found himself considering an America quite different from what Reagan portrayed in his "Let's Make America Great Again" campaign. More than he ever had, Springsteen was contemplating the role of the entertainer. If Reagan's America was a false construction, what truths did it conceal? And who should fight to expose all that was hidden from view?

It was an old question that returned when history demanded it be so: Should the people onstage *extend* their roles? *Nebraska* would unearth images of an America more complicated than any Springsteen had thus far envisioned, but the process started with the questions Springsteen was asking himself on the *River*

Tour. Not everyone wanted their favorite musicians to drag politics into the venue. And that included members of the E Street audience. Was there a way to do it that stopped short of saying, "Vote yes on Prop 10"? It was a line Springsteen wanted to understand, so he was looking out there, finding out just who bought those tickets. What were they there for? He knew it was something more than dancing.

On an off night in St. Louis, Springsteen went to the movies alone. Woody Allen's *Stardust Memories* was showing, a film that's become harder to watch with time. But even then it was uncomfortable. Allen is the lead, playing a filmmaker enough like the man himself that viewers assumed a connection between the two. Throughout the film, Allen is badgered by obnoxious, wildly caricatured fans who are after the filmmaker's autograph, validation, attention, time, scent. They're grotesques.

Before the film started that night in St. Louis, at the concession stand in the theater's lobby, a Springsteen fan named Steve Satanovsky, a knows-all-the-words kind of fan, spotted Springsteen standing there in the popcorn line, a rolled-up newspaper under his arm. Of course, neither Springsteen nor Satanovsky had seen the Woody Allen film. Satanovsky, as a fan, seized the moment. He went up to his favorite performer and asked the man to sit with him and his sister. Springsteen said yes. The musician sat between the siblings. Then it was *Stardust Memories.* The fan as parasite.

Well, shit, what was Satanovsky supposed to say then? So he asked Springsteen, the guy lodged between a fan and his sister, very directly, "Is it really that bad?" To which Springsteen said, "No, I don't feel like that so much."

Jane Schapiro, a writer and former girlfriend of Satanovsky's, years later wrote a beautiful remembrance of Satanovsky, in a piece titled "My Friend and Bruce Springsteen." She'd been invited to *Stardust Memories* that night but had passed, a near miss. By the time of her writing in 2007, Satanovsky was dead from complications related to diabetes. He was in midlife when he died. She'd heard the story of *Stardust Memories* directly from Satanovsky and had read Springsteen's recollection of the night in *Musician*.

As Jane Schapiro heard the story from Satanovsky, after the movie Springsteen asked to borrow change to call a cab, and Satanovsky offered to drive him back to his hotel. Springsteen accepted the offer. Then Satanovsky asked if maybe they could swing by the family home to meet the parents. Which Springsteen agreed to. Satanovsky's mother, in a housedress, cut up some watermelon, apparently requesting a little proof that this was indeed Bruce Springsteen. The album cover wasn't enough. She checked his credit card. Yup, it was him. Before leaving, Springsteen gave the woman his mother's phone number, asking if she could call Adele and testify, mother to mother, as to the well-being of a son.

Only Jane Schapiro's account includes a mention of the fact that Satanovsky, on the drive to his family's house, "slipped a bootleg tape of one of Springsteen's concerts into his eight-track player and began to sing." He even asked Springsteen to join him on one song's chorus. For Schapiro, who had watched her friend Steve track Springsteen from *Greetings from Asbury Park* forward, this was "the best part of the story." It's also a fitting example of what happens when an artist, over a period of years, forges with his fans the kind of intimacy Springsteen had.

One would have to guess that Springsteen did his part in the sing-along. Many artists at Springsteen's level wouldn't have gotten in the car. And if they had, surely they would have found a way out of it when the chorus hit. But Springsteen stayed in the car to find out more about the people to whom he'd been singing for so many years.

When Springsteen got off the *River* Tour, with roughly a year of road work completed, he went with most of the band and much of the crew to Clarence Clemons's Hawaii wedding. There he acted as best man. It was as much an end-of-tour party as it was a nuptials ceremony. Steven Van Zandt was not in attendance. That summer EMI had approached Van Zandt about a solo deal, and, as Dave Marsh recalls, the guitar player got to work "as soon as the tour ended." "Steve was Bruce's oldest friend," Marsh writes, "but he was every bit as brash as his buddy was cautious. Burning up with the idea of an album of his own, he set to work on it without waiting for a contract to be signed, which meant without a company to foot the bills for studio time."

In the months ahead, Van Zandt and Springsteen would work together as producers on a second album for Gary U.S. Bonds, but the urgency and focus Van Zandt brought to his own solo work was no doubt a message impossible to miss. While Van Zandt was the only E Street musician to work his way onto Springsteen's production team, it was becoming clear that he had ambitions beyond that and unrelated to his life in the E Street Band. And why not? But like any band watching one of its core members launch a solo career, the E Street Band was surely feeling the shift.

Unlike Van Zandt, Springsteen didn't come home with a need or a burning desire to capitalize on what *The River* had already made possible. There was no rush to the process of becoming whatever it was Bruce Springsteen was meant to be next. Of course, the two men were in very different situations. Van Zandt was crafting and preparing to launch a solo career. Springsteen was an established bandleader about to stumble, inadvertently, into his own version of that same thing.

The River, as a tour and as an album, was a success to contend with. It made its statement. The rock and roll band and the rock and roll show, as things and sounds and meaningful social constructions, weren't ready to sit behind glass at the Smithsonian. Not yet. Springsteen's audiences had voiced their position. So nothing would have made more sense than to go back at it. But something was stopping Springsteen. Even he didn't know exactly what it was. He grasped that with the European leg of the *River* Tour something had shifted, a greater frontier had opened. The game had gotten bigger, spreading across the globe. And he knew that a hit single and a number one album had left a mark. It was a situation to build on, not linger on. The deeper feeling, however, was one of unease, an unease that had little to do with bands.

Because Springsteen's story so often looks like a dream come true—"That record company, Rosie, just gave me a big advance!"—it's sometimes hard to fathom the trouble he felt when things went according to plan. When I asked him about that moment, the sense of arrival that came with *The River*, he said this:

I knew that something had happened to me that hadn't happened to anyone else I knew. I was a guy that when I first made a record I didn't know anyone else who'd made a record. I'd never met another recording artist. I was totally on my own turf, having my own experience. The main thing that did happen to me when I came off *The River* is that I was solvent, which would make me unique in my little neighborhood. And that was where I still lived. So I was dealing with that, with all my very conflicted feelings about being so separate from the people that I'd grown up around and that I wrote about. I was trying to figure out how I was gonna deal with that. And it was with a lot of guilt for a long time.

Home from Hawaii, Springsteen took his unease back to the Colts Neck rental he'd moved into during the year of the *River* Tour. He got the place after being forced to leave the Holmdel, New Jersey, farmhouse where he'd written *Darkness on the Edge of Town* and *The River*. As Peter Ames Carlin writes, "When Bruce moved from Holmdel to a rented ranch house on the edge of a reservoir in Colts Neck, an exurban area ten minutes east of Freehold, [his then girlfriend Joyce] Hyser helped him to furnish the place by cruising the neighborhoods around Monmouth County on garbage day in search of cast-off chairs and tables." He'd had a number one album and a top ten single, but if you threw out a chair in Colts Neck, New Jersey, in 1981, there was a chance it might end up in Bruce Springsteen's living room.

It wasn't that Springsteen hadn't experienced money. But he was a guy unaccustomed to seeing it go into his bank account and remain there. Some big checks had been in his hands, but they always seemed just to be passing through, on their way to someone else's wallet. That included a check for $800,000 made out to Bruce Springsteen from CBS Records, a check that had had him saying, "I'm a millionaire!" knowing full well he wasn't. He understood without question that by late that day all $800,000 would be used to buy his former manager, Mike Appel, out of the contract that kept Springsteen bound to the man. And, really, it might have been easier for Springsteen to see the money go elsewhere. Then it could be someone else's problem. His discomfort with the trappings of success was no act, more a symptom of his disconnection from his own experiences, past and present.

Springsteen had started the *River* Tour with a total of twenty thousand dollars to his name. That wasn't boat money, horse money, or even car money. It was rent money. By the time the tour ended in Cincinnati, however, things were somewhat different. Somewhat. He was able to reward himself with his first-ever new car, a Camaro Z28. That was about it. And even the Z28 was more an object of shame than it was a symbol of victory. "I felt as conspicuous as if I were driving a solid-gold Rolls-Royce," he'd write in his memoir.

"I sat around and anguished over whether I should spend ten thousand dollars on a *new* car," he recalled. "I was thirty-one and I'd never owned a new car in my life. For that matter, outside of studio expenses, I'd never spent ten thousand dollars on myself. I didn't know anyone who was making more than they could live on." The Camaro was less an experience of celebration than something to manage. And the passenger seat was empty. The moorings for rock and rollers, if somewhat juvenile, were pretty straightforward: What band are you in and who's your girlfriend?

Joyce Hyser had helped Springsteen move in, had in fact been his girlfriend since 1978, but the relationship was over by the end of the *River* Tour, and she all but evaporated from the story. As she told Carlin, "His whole thing in those days was, 'When I want to see you, you need to be here, and when I don't, you need to be gone.'" Now it was a deeper kind of gone. Dave Marsh's definitive biography makes one mention of Hyser, spelling her name "Heiser" and giving her a bit part in an anecdote about Robin Williams.

No girlfriend, the band scattered, alone. That was Springsteen's predicament in the fall of 1981. Though one crew member had described Springsteen's life during the writing of *Darkness on the Edge of Town,* several years earlier, as "his loner period," people have said the same of other times in Springsteen's life. But none of those "loner periods" were as pronounced as the months following the *River* Tour. "It was definitely a closing to a certain earlier section in my life," Springsteen told Carlin. "The initial section of the traveling and touring and those early records."

"He was back to being a full-time loner," writes Dave Marsh, adding that "now the loner was beginning to experience his condition in a different way—as nothing more than loneliness." Sitting with him in 2021, I asked him about that moment, about that house that was not a home.

WZ: Thinking of the Holmdel farmhouse you were in before that, where you worked on *Darkness, The River*— there the band was the family. So your experience coming off the *River* Tour is . . . well, you hadn't come home to a house that empty in a while.

SPRINGSTEEN: Right, and that's what I did.

WZ: And you were coming out of a relationship.

SPRINGSTEEN: Yes, that's right. I was really on my own. The house I had been in, the big farmhouse, was very . . . it was a very inclusive space, a big rambling old farmhouse. And I sort of did an emergency landing coming out of *The River*, got thrown out of that farmhouse and ended up renting a ranch house which was not much of a house at all. But I made the record there.

At night he'd drive the "solid gold" Camaro to Freehold, going to see the homes where he'd lived with his grandparents and parents. He never got out of the car. It was what he describes as a "pathetic and quasi-religious compulsion." "My car was my sealed time capsule," he explains in *Born to Run,* "from whose bucket seats I could experience the little town that had its crushing boot on my neck in whatever mental time, space or moment I chose. Come evening I rolled through its streets, listening for the voices of my father, my mother, me as a child." No sound of a crowd, just ghosts and anxious murmurs.

From that point forward Springsteen would never again be in a band the way he'd been in one for *The River.* He was not someone's boyfriend, didn't even belong in his own neighborhood. He was alone and in *Nebraska.* "He kind of went into seclusion," Max Weinberg, drummer in the E Street Band, recalled to Brian Hiatt. "You didn't see a lot of him, and for a while none of us even knew where he lived. I remember that distinctly."

CHAPTER SIX

Other People's Titles

After they laughed at me a few times, they began requesting the hillbilly stuff.

—CHUCK BERRY

In Springsteen's recollection, the first song that came was "Mansion on the Hill." Exactly when the song was started is the subject of differing accounts. It seems fragments of "Mansion on the Hill" had appeared even a few years earlier, in a notebook from the *Darkness on the Edge of Town* period. But it was really just images not yet framed within a story, strays waiting for a home. As he later described to Don McLeese, the writing process went quickly after that:

> I was home for only a month, and I started to write all those songs. I wrote 'em real fast. Two months, the whole record, and for me that's real quick. I just sat at my desk, and it was something that was really fascinating for me. It was one of those times when you're not really thinking

about it. You're working on it, but you're doing something that you didn't think you would be doing. I knew I wanted to make a certain type of record, but I certainly didn't plan to make that record.

There was a noteworthy thing done with "Mansion on the Hill," and it wasn't for the first time. Springsteen grabbed an existing title and built a song around it. Of course, it wasn't "Hey Jude" or "Night Moves" that he lifted. His appropriation found Springsteen planting a foot in a particular past, a more distant and decidedly southern past, where so much American music has found its character and longing. He'd done it once before, with *The River*'s "Wreck on the Highway."

Neither of the titles Springsteen borrowed are obscurities. And his "theft" wasn't some clandestine act. It was all done out in the open, more a declaration of lineage than anything else. Springsteen had spoken freely about his growing interest in country music, particularly in the years immediately preceding *Nebraska*. He felt a connection, forged in his earliest years, to the rural life that animated so much country music.

"In those days, in my childhood, there was town and country," he told me. "Nothing in the middle. There were no suburbs. You either lived in town or in the country. We were very close to the agricultural life, partly because my grandfather dealt with migrant workers who came up from the South. He sold them radios and things that he pulled out of the trash. It was a different world. But those things, town and country, felt much closer together then." Country music reconnected him with that, those song titles to a world no longer there. To step into one of those titles, as a songwriter, was to wear another man's clothing. And the men from whom he borrowed them interested Springsteen, their shadowlike presence.

The River's "Wreck on the Highway" got its title from a song written by Dorsey Dixon in 1937 and made famous by Roy Acuff, who claimed it as his own until Dixon eventually lawyered up. In the years following Acuff's release, "Wreck on the Highway" became something of a standard in country and bluegrass. For its part, "Mansion on the Hill" had its antecedent in a Hank Williams's cut by the name "A Mansion on the Hill," credited to Williams and the publisher Fred Rose and recorded early in Williams's brief but remarkable career.

The writing of Hank Williams's "A Mansion on the Hill" reveals the particularities of country songwriting culture as distinct from, say, 1970s singer-songwriter traditions. There was often nothing overly mystical about song creation in country culture. Wesley Rose, Fred's son, claims that Hank Williams showed up in his father's world just as father and son were playing a game of Ping-Pong. In an effort to make sure Hank Williams was indeed the writer of the songs he was presenting, which Rose recognized as decidedly strong material, Fred Rose asked Williams to write something on the spot. Rose gave him a theme to work with, which Colin Escott describes as "a woman leaves the one she truly loves to marry a man with money." Williams came back to Fred Rose with "A Mansion on the Hill." Fred Rose got the co-writing credit and signed the artist of a lifetime. They worked in the song business, and that was just one of the thousand ways a song could come into being.

Escott challenges the veracity of Wesley Rose's version of the song's origin story, however, and also provides an alternate account, this one from Hank Williams's widow, Audrey. In Audrey Williams's recollection, Fred Rose gave Hank Williams the title "A Mansion on the Hill," and Williams took it home to turn it into a song. The aim was the same, however: a chance for Williams to prove his talent. But the great Hank Williams was stuck, Audrey insists, until she helped him find his way. Uncredited.

As Escott goes on to explain, if Williams got the title from Fred Rose, he poached the melody from Bob Wills. It was the kind of stuff that happened all the time. Themes, titles, melodies: the point wasn't to do anything but find a song, even if it happened to be in another's purse. The unique utterance of the individual artist, the song as a confession from the soul? Those were ideas belonging to another world of popular music. The culture of country music, like that of early blues and gospel, wasn't precious about the process of songwriting. The near idolatry associated with the voice of the individual songwriter is more a thing of the late 1960s and the 1970s, of a world associated with Joni Mitchell, James Taylor, and others. In country music you could steal things in the night and know you'd probably meet others out there doing the same thing.

In grabbing a title off the shelf, "Mansion on the Hill," Springsteen was aligning himself with another tradition of songwriters and songwriting, where words and melodies and titles were out there for repossession and figures like Dorsey Dixon could slip from view into a kind of obscurity while their songs carried on without them. No rock stars in that world, just a lot of sequins and rhinestones on workers' backs. Anonymity was always close by, and "artists" were people who made paintings and sculptures.

While his bandmate and, more recently, co-producer, Steven Van Zandt, was off looking to add "front man" to his résumé, Springsteen was alone in New Jersey trying to disappear, to be anonymous in some way, a Dorsey Dixon. His ambivalence about celebrity, or at least his lack of trust in it, was more alive than at any other point in his career. He felt as if he no longer belonged with the people he grew up with and wrote about, but neither did he feel at home where he'd ended up, as a celebrity.

There was, as he told me, "a lot of strange stuff in the air." So he wanted, he said, "to be invisible." There was some effect, when songwriting inside another songwriter's title, of wearing not just another man's clothes but a mask. It wasn't invisibility, but it was close. It was certainly the right place to start an invisibility project. "Mansion on the Hill" set that up, created a place to begin, whether Springsteen was thinking he was beginning something or not.

In a 1981 *Musician* interview with Dave Marsh, Springsteen, on the cusp of making *Nebraska,* describes his interest in southern music from back then and "out there":

I went back and dug up all the early rockabilly stuff because . . . what mysterious people they were.

There's this song, "Jungle Rock" by Hank Mizell. Where is Hank Mizell? What happened to him? What a mysterious person, what a ghost. And you put that thing on and you can see him. You can see him standing in some little studio, way back when, and just singing that song. No reason [*laughs*]. Nothing gonna come of it. Didn't sell. That wasn't no Number One record, and he wasn't playin' no big arena after it, either.

But what a moment, what a mythic moment, what a mystery. Those records are filled with mystery. Like these wild men came out from somewhere, and man, they were so alive. The joy and the abandon.

As if in response to the unease and disconnection he felt in relation to his own success with *The River,* Springsteen was drawn to the "wild men" of American music, these ghosts, forgotten and historically distant figures he found to be "filled with mystery." The ones who left a mark without ever knowing success. "Wreck on the Highway" and "Mansion on the Hill," titles taken from others, brought Springsteen closer to their worlds.

When I asked him about what was going on there, Springsteen said, "I could see that something different was happening, but I didn't think a lot about it. I loved that music, was listening to it, of course, but there wasn't some greater purpose there in using those titles, nothing conscious. It just happened." But that circuit he took through a particular past in American music did forge a connectedness to the world of "hillbilly music" and a rural, poor American past that would breathe throughout *Nebraska.* Even if Springsteen's mansion had a Freehold address.

Some years later, introducing "Mansion on the Hill" during a show, Springsteen described childhood car rides taken through

Freehold with his father. "At night my pop would take me and we'd all ride in the car. And we would drive around the town," he said. "It was funny, we'd lived there, always, but yet we'd go sightseeing. And he'd always drive past the nice big houses and it always seemed really mystical. I did not understand what those people had to do with me or my dad or who we were."

The theme that Fred Rose had passed along to Hank Williams for "A Mansion on the Hill"—"a woman leaves the one she truly loves to marry a man with money"—is far from Springsteen's "Mansion on the Hill." Williams's lost love story, with the man looking from his cabin up toward the "loveless mansion on the hill," hits a few old notes, like money can't buy happiness and "real" life is on the poor side of "town." Differently, Springsteen's "Mansion on the Hill" doesn't yield to either sentimentality or easy morality. And most important, the point of view that matters the most in Springsteen's version is that of the child, living in a world before romance and class begin to reorganize life:

> At night my daddy'd take me and we'd ride
> Through the streets of a town so silent and still
> Park on a back road along the highway side
> Look up at that mansion on the hill
>
> In the summer all the lights would shine
> There'd be music playing, people laughing all the time
> Me and my sister we'd hide out in the tall corn fields
> Sit and listen to the mansion on the hill

What's absent is any trace of judgment. The world of the children, hidden in the cornfields, isn't presented as more or less pure than the world of music and laughter they hear in the distant mansion. And the splendor above doesn't become an easy symbol of greed. The scene may as well be from a fairy tale, removed from any historical context. Steel gates surround the mansion, but no point of view forces a reading that makes one side of those gates good and the other bad.

"I think that if an adult is singing about class," the songwriter Dave Alvin says of the song, "it can come across as dogmatic, where if a child paints the picture, there's that sense of wonder. It draws out something even deeper. I'm sure that's among the reasons that song affected me as it did. I could feel his deep emotional attachment to his subject matter."

Matt Berninger of the National describes a similar feeling about the child's point of view and how it functions in relation to "Mansion on the Hill":

> How many people in this country have nothing while a few other people have 99 percent of all wealth and re-sources? That idea of a mansion on the hill, of *having* one of them, is potent and finds a lot of people slaving away so there can be the one guy with that house. That's what America is like. That's the toxification of this American dream. We have enough resources here for everyone, but as long as we're all dreaming of the mansion . . . shit. But we think about it differently when it's seen through a child's eyes. That perspective puts us in a more ambiguous place. That point of view in the song helps us get at something

way beyond a black-and-white reading of the American dream.

"I was definitely interested in complexity, human complexity, and not being judgmental," Springsteen told me. "I just wanted it to be presentational. I didn't have an ax to grind, certainly not on that record."

As the songs started to arrive, it would become clear that even the most troubled characters of *Nebraska* would stand beyond the reach of a simple moral scrutiny. That wasn't the theater in which they were players. The song world they inhabited didn't lead to easy sorting, good and bad. But the point of view of the child, driven more by curiosity and wonder than by judgment, doesn't just provide a way out of that sorting; it also gets Springsteen into the world of his own childhood. "Mansion on the Hill" has that dreamlike quality. The temporality of the song is fluid not fixed. By the final verse, it may be that the speaker has grown up, but it's debatable. The voice floats through the song. It set a tone for a record rooted in Springsteen's childhood.

Where, Springsteen asked himself at the end of the *River* Tour, did he belong? Was it where he came from, a poor home in Freehold, or where he was going to, a success well beyond any reasonable expectations? As he would come to discover through the process of letting the songs arrive quickly and without a plan, the *Nebraska* material was going to press on this unanswerable question, offering no relief from the in-betweenness of it all. The songs took Springsteen back yet kept him apart from the people he found there. The solitary drives he was taking, like some reenactment of those childhood car rides with his father, opened onto something that had been put away. "The ghosts of *Nebraska,*" he would write, "were drawn from my many sojourns into the small-town streets I'd grown up on."

It meant that the material on *Nebraska* would be more connected to Springsteen's childhood than that on any other album. "'Mansion on the Hill' was just a childhood recollection," he said, "but it allowed me to address the conflicts I was feeling." When I asked Springsteen whether he felt himself to be outside the steel gates or inside them at the time of writing, he answered without hesitation: "I felt like I was in both places. And in the very near future I was going to be spending a lot of time trying to reconcile that."

That song opened onto a very particular landscape. But the next song he wrote, "Nebraska," would be the one that began to populate that landscape with characters. When he got to that second song—and it came on the heels of "Mansion on the Hill"—Springsteen says that he'd "found the record's center." And that's when it went from "mystical," to use Springsteen's word, to dark and troubled.

WZ: Freud's therapeutic model involves going back to childhood to understand the tangles of adulthood. It seems you were an intuitively therapeutic person.

SPRINGSTEEN: That was my nature.

WZ: But you're supposed to do it with somebody, supposed to have a guide with you.

SPRINGSTEEN: I didn't have that down yet. I didn't figure that part out yet. That came later.

WZ: Soon.

SPRINGSTEEN: Very soon. But I wasn't quite ready to be with someone in that way, not at that point in my life. I was a little young still. Culturally it still wasn't looked on all that fondly. My first years with analysis I had to sneak in and out. I was very self-conscious about it for a long time. So, no, I wasn't there yet.

CHAPTER SEVEN

Any Kind of Life?

I've always believed the greatest rock and roll musicians are desperate men.

—Bruce Springsteen on Elvis Costello's *Spectacle*

f at the end of the *River* Tour Bruce Springsteen entered a period of heightened self-investigation, it wasn't that the world of his interior had been locked up and hidden from view until that point. True to the emotional character of the music he'd made, he'd approached interviews with a consistent openness for years. He'd certainly said enough to suggest to his public that he knew ambivalence, that he wasn't even sure, as he had been early on, that rock and roll could save souls. It had started in the aftermath of *Born to Run*. By the time of a 1978 *King Biscuit Flower Hour* interview, conducted during the *Darkness on the Edge of Town* tour, Springsteen didn't hesitate to express the kinds of doubts that were growing inside him.

The featured *King Biscuit Flower Hour* interviews went long, almost like the radio version of a *Rolling Stone* artist interview.

For the FM audience, it was something to listen to, to tape, to talk about. The program's name played on that of a legendary radio program out of the American South, *King Biscuit Time.* The latter first aired in 1941, coming out of Helena, Arkansas, and featuring Sonny Boy Williamson and Robert Lockwood Jr. From 1951 forward its host was "Sunshine" Sonny Payne, who would start the program declaring, "Pass the biscuits, 'cause it's King Biscuit Time!" In those days the sponsor got its nod right up front, nothing quiet about it.

King Biscuit Time was a significant megaphone for the Delta Blues, reaching a wide audience that included the likes of B. B. King, Levon Helm, and hundreds of others who were going to make something from what they heard. In 1973, the show's name was adopted and adapted, given a hippie slant, as the *King Biscuit Flower Hour.* The first program featured Blood, Sweat & Tears, the Mahavishnu Orchestra, and a young Bruce Springsteen playing Max's Kansas City. It was just after Springsteen's debut release.

Five years later, when Springsteen again appeared on the *King Biscuit Flower Hour,* this time for an extended interview with the WNEW deejay Dave Herman, the show was a rock radio staple. The black part of the *King Biscuit* story, however, was almost entirely obscured, there only in the impact it had on many of the white guest artists raised on R&B, blues, and soul music. The cultural revolution of the 1960s, which rock music had done so much to promote, claimed victories difficult to sustain. The programming on the *King Biscuit Flower Hour* was mostly male, mostly white, and included multiple appearances by Foreigner.

The interviews on the show, however, went long and deep.

In the 1978 Springsteen interview he comes off as unguarded and thoughtful, if a little weary. As a document, it captures the Bruce Springsteen of the *Darkness on the Edge of Town* era as well as anything.

Columbia announced *Darkness on the Edge of Town* a full two years before the album's actual release. Of course, there was shit going down in those few years: Springsteen was settling the lawsuit with his former manager, Mike Appel, which would eventually release him from a contract that had him in a financial and creative bind; was engaged in extreme artistic indecision and second-guessing in the studio; and, as the interview reveals, was facing what could only be called a growing personal anxiety, an anxiety that would finally get on record with *Nebraska*.

Describing to Dave Herman the sense of possibility he felt as a kid in his first rock and roll bands, Springsteen says, "I found something that was like a key to a little door that said there's more to it than this." For years, he insists, he was "living out [his] rock and roll dream." The limits of that dream, and the weariness of the 1978 interview, are most palpable, however, when Springsteen references *Born to Run* and the hype surrounding it, which would lead to his initial *refusal* to promote its follow-up, *Darkness on the Edge of Town*. He'd made contact with the dream early but by *Born to Run* "felt that slipping away." He was experiencing what he described as "the old gas pedal stuck to the floor, in a runaway car."

He'd said things like this before, but there's something more in his voice when he gets to that "slipping away" part. As Dave Marsh shares in *Two Hearts,* it was only a few years into Springsteen's recording career when the musician was saying of himself, "I eat loneliness, man." By the time of the *King Biscuit* interview, if the message was the same it had lost any trace of the heroic tone.

> **DAVE HERMAN:** Bruce, do you have like any kind of life that is totally divorced from music? Do you have anything when you're not working or, I mean like you're not recording, you're not on the road . . . do you do anything that's got nothing to do with rock and roll?
>
> **SPRINGSTEEN:** No, just . . . I don't think I do. Trying to think.
>
> **DH:** Your friends are all in . . .
>
> **SPRINGSTEEN:** I've had girlfriends. In general, I've got one friend that's not really involved in the music business and he owns a motorcycle shop in Westwood . . . Town and Country Cycle. And there's a little plug there I guess, his name is Matty. And I guess he's my only friend that doesn't work for me, or is not involved in some other way.

When the rock and roll part was stripped away, there wasn't a lot left. It was a little like the middle of nowhere.

Springsteen can be an unforgiving judge of his own work, as if he's still scrutinizing the recordings upon which his legacy is built. *Born to Run* he'll now describe as "young," saying that he can't listen to it comfortably. *Born in the U.S.A.* he'll say surprises him in its success, that he never felt entirely sure about it. But there's no hesitation with *Nebraska*. There he's unwavering.

Talking about it with me at his Colts Neck home, he repeatedly pointed in the direction of the rental where the album was made, almost as if he could see the place from where we were sitting. I kept looking when he pointed. "Hundred years from now, what's gonna play well?" he said. "That record will play pretty well. It's just one of those records. If people are interested, that represents a particular place and time. It has a particular view of America and tells a particular kind of story. That record will always stand up. It'll always hold up."

Rare are the recordings that come of the kind of isolation Springsteen was experiencing. One has to consider what, in all that isolation, *was* speaking to Springsteen when people weren't.

There are times in most any artist's career when they're absorbing more, searching for and sorting through more, not always knowing why they're doing so. For *Nebraska,* Springsteen had found some "unforgivingness" in Suicide that inspired him. Country music had given him a rural connection, a sense of place and of outsiders, a rough, working-class American past. Most of the searching and sorting, though, didn't involve music. More than any other record he made, *Nebraska* was one that he would later explain with reference to a strangely specific list of inspirations and source materials. Most of it had some connection to the 1950s of his childhood; all of it had characters and settings that carried traces of the same "unforgivingness" he found in Suicide.

If *Nebraska* was a mystery of sorts, the clues given to understand it were these: Charles Laughton's film *The Night of the Hunter,* Flannery O'Connor's short stories, Robert Frank's book of photographs *The Americans,* and, most conspicuously, Terrence Malick's *Badlands.*

CHAPTER EIGHT

The Record's Center

There will frequently occur gaps, in the long winter evenings, that are hard to fill up satisfactorily, hours when, tired of reading or study, a boy does not know what to do.

—D. C. BEARD, *The American Boy's Handy Book,* 1882

That fall in 1981, Springsteen was spending a lot of time alone in the Colts Neck rental. The orange shag carpets made it seem all the more like someone else's place. Sometimes he'd write songs. Sometimes he'd get back from Freehold and watch TV by himself late into the night. Flipping through the channels on one of those solitary evenings, he found *Badlands,* the Terrence Malick film loosely based on the 1958 Charles Starkweather murder spree. In the same way that Suicide's "Frankie Teardrop" spoke to him, Malick's film pushed its way into Springsteen's chest. Something about that story of a teenage serial murderer reminded Springsteen of his own life.

Years before, he'd written a song called "Badlands." Maybe he was wondering what another artist, this time a filmmaker, would do with the same title. Maybe not. Maybe there was nothing else on. Maybe he didn't like what came into his mind when the television was off. Either way, Malick's *Badlands* had a mood and violence that struck Springsteen. It clung to him. It was still there in the morning.

It wasn't a pay-per-view or a streaming world at that time. When you came upon something on the television, it was more like "a discovery," a thing stumbled upon in the night. *Badlands* was released in 1973, the same year as *Greetings from Asbury Park;* it just took a little time for the movie and the man to find each other. But it's Malick's film where *Nebraska* gets its foundation in trouble. As a testament to the film's role as a source and inspiration, there's a fragment of it in the very first lines of the *Nebraska* album. That baton in the first verse of the song "Nebraska" comes straight out of actress Sissy Spacek's hands. "I saw her standing / on her front lawn / just a twirlin' / her baton." A handoff.

Badlands isn't some buried reference. "Mansion on the Hill" could have opened onto a multitude of full-length albums, but once "Nebraska" arrived, a song that Springsteen found in the space between where he was sitting and the television screen, the album got its direction and its darkness, its spiritual recklessness. The characters of *Nebraska,* like Charles Starkweather, often faced, in Springsteen's words, the "thin line between stability and that moment when time stops and everything goes to black."

There's another movie belonging to the *Nebraska* period that carries within it some of the themes and ideas and conflict Springsteen works with throughout *Nebraska: Raging Bull,*

Martin Scorsese and Robert De Niro's great collaboration released in 1980. That film, like *Nebraska,* is a study of human violence and deprivation, with a rigorous aesthetic grounded in black and white. The unchecked, animal impulses of the boxer Jake LaMotta bear distinct resemblance to those of Charles Starkweather, despite differences in place, culture, context. But for Springsteen, *Raging Bull* is missing something that, as he explained to me, helps one to better understand what was crucial to him at the time and why *Badlands* was the one:

> I love [*Raging Bull*]. And I guess if you were going to ask if *Nebraska* is color or black and white, you'd naturally say black and white. But I don't remember *Raging Bull* having a huge influence on that particular record. The films that mattered to *Nebraska* were really quiet pieces. The way that they landed in the culture. They were silent. *Badlands* was a pretty quiet event when it came out. It didn't make that big splash. I remember it got some attention, but it didn't make that big splash. And that connected up with the kind of place I was in. I was drawing from culturally quiet places and sources.

Part of what mattered to Springsteen was the way the film approached him, late at night, by chance, like some unexpected knock at the door. Scorsese's *Raging Bull* was an event. *Badlands* was not. Springsteen's ambivalence about big career success, which he'd wanted, fought for, and feared, drew him toward art that mattered and lasted, without ever being a hit, a blockbuster, a thing of red carpets and flashbulbs.

Malick's film came out in 1973, a Warner Bros. release. Scorsese's earlier *Mean Streets* and William Friedkin's *Exorcist* were among the studio's other offerings that same year. Only the last of them, Friedkin's, made a dent in the marketplace. *Badlands* had a limited theatrical run, over time making its way, without much fanfare, to late-night television. But for Springsteen, the way in which *Badlands* stayed in quiet circulation resulted in a kind of Hank Mizell effect. Terrence Malick followed up *Badlands* with *Days of Heaven,* then disappeared for some twenty years. He wouldn't do interviews; there were even questions about what he looked like. Relative to the workings of Hollywood, he was, as Springsteen described Hank Mizell, the voice behind "Jungle Rock," a wild man and a mystery both. *That* interested Springsteen.

But there was also a looseness to *Badlands,* an aspect that couldn't be found in a script or storyboards, that appealed to Springsteen. If *Raging Bull* was a work of mastery, in its editing, acting, and directing, *Badlands* seemed almost to wander in search of itself, without hiding this from the viewer. When interviewed for *Elvis Presley: The Searcher,* Springsteen describes a similar, compelling looseness when speaking of Presley's earliest recording sessions for Sam Phillips's Sun Records in Memphis. All that Springsteen says of those sessions could be applied to the making of Terrence Malick's *Badlands:* "Not knowing quite where they're going to go. Not knowing exactly what they're doing. Just discovering and doing it, literally as the music is being played. You're out on the frontier, and it's a very pristine and exciting place to be."

Malick's classmate and collaborator Jake Brackman said of the *Badlands* production and the film's director, "Members of the crew were constantly making jack-off gestures behind Terry's back. Sissy [Spacek] and Martin [Sheen] were the only people who thought he knew what he was doing." The assistant cameraman Tony Palmieri and others would insist that unknowingness was crucial, or at least inescapable, when it came to the making of *Badlands.* "I don't think any of us on the crew," Palmieri said, "really knew what the fuck we were doing." If they did know, it seems they quit.

The assistant director Bill Scott agrees. "We were so green. A couple years ago, Terry told me that on that first morning of filming, after he got his big wide shot, the cameraman turned to him and said, 'Should we go in for coverage now, Terry?' And Terry said, 'No, let's do an over-the-shoulder shot'— which *is* coverage. And I remember when someone asked me if I had ordered the honey wagon, I said, 'Yeah, the catering's all lined up.' The honey wagon's the toilet truck."

Tony Palmieri would later insist, "Understanding Terrence Malick will probably be impossible. But for thirty-four years, every time I mention *Badlands,* someone's eyebrows go up. They want to know all about it." Some would say the film was glued together with voice-over. Members of the crew would describe fistfights on the set, with even the director landing punches. "They were accustomed to sticking to a plan," Sissy Spacek said about her experience making the film. "That's not the way Terry likes to work."

For the film's two featured actors, Spacek and Martin Sheen, it was their first leading roles in a feature. They didn't challenge the director who gave them the opportunity; they followed him. They had just stepped into their dreams, why step back? Sheen later recalled:

Terry called one night and said, "I want you to play the part." I had to get up very early the next morning to go to work, and I was driving along the Pacific Coast Highway in a little Mazda. I was listening to a Dylan album I was fond of, and the song "Desolation Row" was playing, and the sun was rising, and it hit me that I was going to play the role of my life. I had been a professional actor since I was eighteen. I was thirty-one, I had four children, I was struggling, doing a lot of television—a lot of bad, silly work just to make ends meet—and I wasn't having any luck in features to speak of, and here was the part of my life. And I was overwhelmed, and I pulled off to the side of the road, and I wept uncontrollably.

Prior to landing her role in *Badlands,* Sissy Spacek, a Texan, recorded and released a soon-to-be-forgotten single, "John You Went Too Far This Time," under the name Rainbo. Without a master plan of any substance, she left Texas for New York City. "Just about every town in Texas has a beauty pageant," she recalled. "Ours was called The Dogwood Fiesta. I was in one of those. I played the guitar and sang—and lost. But one of the judges was a newspaper reporter and she was going to New York and my brother was real sick at the time and my parents thought it would be good for me to get out from under that so I came to visit."

In New York, occasionally hanging out at Max's Kansas City, Spacek met the Andy Warhol superstar Holly Woodlawn (the same Holly referenced in the first verse of Lou Reed's "Walk on the Wild Side"). Woodlawn helped Spacek get an extra role in Warhol's film *Trash*. From there Spacek moved to Los Angeles "one suitcase at a time." *Badlands* was her breakthrough. *Coal Miner's Daughter* and *Carrie* would be among the films that would cement her status as one of Hollywood's elite, just as *Apocalypse Now* would bring Sheen to the upper reaches.

With those two actors and Malick, a director making his first feature, there were three people on the *Badlands* set each day realizing long-held dreams, without knowing fully what they were doing. That feeling of arrival, together with the looseness inherent in Malick's approach, made the film all the more like the cinematic version of Elvis's first Sun sessions.

"The shoot went on forever," Sissy Spacek recalled in an interview with *The Guardian*, "because the crew kept quitting. They were completely brutalized. They'd be setting up one shot over here, then Terry would look over in the other direction where the moon was rising up and he'd go, 'Let's shoot over there!' I have these memories of everyone tearing off across the desert in pursuit of one sunset or another."

By most accounts Malick was a kind of visual obsessive. He put the light before the narrative, if only because he believed that light had a way of telling some of the best stories. Springsteen would later describe *Nebraska* in terms that echo Malick's priorities, revealing another connection between Springsteen and the film. "Light," he told me as we discussed Malick's film and its impact on the recordings he would make in Colts Neck. "That was my judgment on the entire success of *Nebraska*." It was as if Malick's film helped Springsteen to think of his songs as filmmakers and photographers might think of their images. And it wouldn't just change the nature of his writing and singing; it would alter his understanding of how records could *sound*.

That looseness, that light, whether in *Badlands* or in Presley's first Sun sessions, was a thing you might get to only once in your career. It happens quickly in an artist's trajectory that they begin to know too much to know so little again. For his own part, Springsteen had been there as a young record maker, and some part of him was determined to get back there again—no matter that he was five albums into a major career.

The spontaneity of early creations, the time before things get "big": it was all there in *Badlands* as Springsteen watched, alone in his rented home. And then, of course, there was the story. A murder spree. In that, somehow, he saw his childhood.

CHAPTER NINE

Blood in Black and White

Blood, sex, melodrama and crime have always been big
sellers. In the early days of television, a sense of respectabil-
ity modeled on the printed press kept these attention-
grabbers under wraps, but the race for audience share
inevitably brings it to the headlines and to the beginning of
the television news.

—PIERRE BOURDIEU, *On Television*

"Mansion on the Hill," with its floating point of view, hovering between the worlds of the haves and the have-nots, was for Springsteen a gateway into the world of his childhood, but "Nebraska" was a way into its trauma. He wrote an early version of the song in the third person, then titled "Starkweather." As the song evolved, however, it became a first-person account, Springsteen and Charles Starkweather sharing a voice, a story. That change in point of view was as telling as anything. The song would open the album and determine the emotional character of the project.

Like Terrence Malick, the writer Stephen King, and the director Peter Jackson, Springsteen was drawn to Charles Starkweather's story. But among them, only Springsteen took on the first-person point of view in bringing Starkweather into his art.

Springsteen would sing from the electric chair. It would be jarring for fans who considered all of his work confessional in nature. What was he confessing to now, and why?

The Starkweather murder spree made the unthinkable thinkable for many Americans in January 1958. Starkweather killed ten people in the days between January 21 and January 28, and one more, a gas station attendant, in the month before. He killed innocent people, teenagers, a baby. The role of his accomplice, Caril Ann Fugate, whose mother, stepfather, and infant half sister were among those murdered, would remain in question. The spree was the first such serial killings to be told as a television news story. In 1950, less than 10 percent of American homes had televisions. By 1958? About 90 percent. It was through television that Starkweather and Fugate met their audience.

The random nature of the killings and Starkweather's disconnected, ambivalent, sometimes cavalier position regarding his violent crimes helped make him an object of collective fascination. His father, Guy Starkweather, told the courts that when he'd take his son hunting, the young man would continue to shoot animals long after they were dead.

Jeff McArthur, the grandson of Caril Ann Fugate's attorney, John McArthur, writes in his book *Pro Bono: The 18-Year Defense of Caril Ann Fugate* that Starkweather "sat at the table often with a smile on his face." "This was," McArthur continues, "the most attention he had ever received in his life, and it was worth cutting that life short for these few days of infamy." When Starkweather's attorneys pressured him to go with an insanity plea, Starkweather resisted. "Nobody remembers a crazy man," he said. He worked, instead, on his look, to the degree that the penal system allowed. *That* people would remember, as the words of the younger McArthur confirm: "He was almost the spitting image of James Dean, but with bright red hair."

But Starkweather wasn't the spitting image of James Dean. Starkweather was bowlegged, the result of a birth defect, with proportions in body and face that tilted away from received ideas of beauty. He had a speech impediment that had made school days hell and had a knack for bringing up the rear at work. "He was the dumbest man we had," said one former supervisor.

Charles Starkweather wasn't a guy made for the leading man part. Not without the cameras and an audience ready to project onto him attributes that didn't belong to him. For Starkweather to have a chance in a James Dean look-alike contest, the cameras would need to cooperate. But the cameras *would* cooperate. And so would the audience looking at the serial killer. "It made the country step back," Martin Sheen would remark, "and say, 'We're more into image than reality, and this guy is a reflection of that.'"

Through some twisted process, Charles Starkweather crossed over from struggle and invisibility into notoriety and even a kind of charisma. He went out a star. He put on a good show before they threw the switch. This was the man whose voice Springsteen took on in "Nebraska."

The day after watching *Badlands,* Springsteen was thinking about Malick's film and wanting to know more. It wouldn't be on television again that next night. At the library, he found a book, *Caril,* a biography of Starkweather's accomplice written by Ninette Beaver, B. K. Ripley, and Patrick Trese. Ninette Beaver had been part of Omaha's KMTV news team, the station that first reported the Starkweather story in 1958. Before anyone else was given the chance, she interviewed Caril Ann Fugate immediately after the killings.

In *Caril* one reads about the murders but also hears of the Omaha news team grappling with a new medium. KMTV's film gear had arrived only weeks before the Starkweather murder spree. Most KMTV team members didn't know how to use it, or if they did, how to tell stories with it. No one at the time thought television news would ever challenge the dominance of newspapers. Even as they were struggling with the cameras, however, the 1958 KMTV staff got a sense that Caril Ann Fugate would in fact be as much of an object of interest to their viewers as Starkweather was. Possibly more.

As recalled in *Caril,* "Floyd [Kalber of KMTV] called his staff together and outlined his plan of attack. 'This is the biggest murder story to hit this country in a long time,' he said. 'And it's different. Usually what we want to know is whether the defendant is guilty or not. But not this time. Charlie's been confessing to anyone who'll stand still long enough to listen. Now we're going to find out what he's been saying about the murders. And also, what part the girl played. That's what the people want to know, and that's what we're going to report.'"

Though Caril Ann Fugate was fourteen years old at the time of the murders and courtroom proceedings, she would be tried as an adult. Ninette Beaver's sympathy for Fugate, her ultimate belief in Fugate's innocence and sense that this was a child in an adult hell, drove Beaver to connect with the girl, who was ultimately responsive. But before meeting with and interviewing Fugate, Beaver conducted her first on-camera interview as a television reporter with Charles Starkweather's parents. The interview took place in the dining room of the Starkweather family home, just after the accused murderer's parents returned from visiting their now infamous son in lockdown. The Starkweathers weren't sure where they should look. Right at the cameras? Those things were supposed to be pointed at Gary Cooper and Marilyn Monroe. In Hollywood, not Nebraska.

For Ninette Beaver's interview with Caril Ann Fugate, Fugate's attorneys agreed to a filmed conversation prior to the accused's hearing, but only on the condition that all questions from the assembled members of the press went through Beaver. The other assembled press would be in the room, but they'd be writing their questions down for the KMTV reporter to present. Almost as soon as the event commenced, however, Beaver knew this press conference would not help the girl's cause. "Ninette began her questions," the authors of *Caril* recount. "She was shocked by the way Caril responded. The friendly little girl she had met just a few minutes before answered in a clipped, brittle voice. She had changed into a hard-faced, angry young woman." Fugate, as untutored as Starkweather's parents, thought that's what she was supposed to do when a camera was on her. But she chose the wrong version of herself. She was trying to be an adult. And those who were bent on telling a story of Fugate's guilt had exactly what they needed.

Public sympathy for Caril Ann Fugate would fluctuate contingent on the image she projected. Her attorneys were furious when Caril's hair was cut short in custody, robbing her of a girlish look. The vacillations would be wrenching for Fugate, child to adult, adult to child, victim to killer, killer to victim. Early on, when Fugate was in the custody of a sheriff, the sheriff's wife had to break the news to Fugate that her mother, stepfather, and infant stepsister were indeed among the murdered. The woman handed Caril Ann Fugate tissues when she started crying. "When Caril was all out of tears," Jeff McArthur writes, "she began twisting the tissues into the shapes of tiny dolls." But the public didn't get to see the tiny dolls. That was off camera.

Reading *Caril,* Springsteen was struck by the slippage between the worlds of childhood and adulthood, by the violence, fantasy, celebrity, and the public shaming of the courtroom. He saw that one of the problems Caril Ann Fugate would face was Starkweather's changing story. If at the outset Starkweather declared Fugate's innocence, protecting her, as he neared his own death, that story changed. Dramatically. The romance was gone. "When I go to the electric chair," Starkweather said, "I want Caril Fugate sitting right there on my lap." It's a line of Starkweather's that would find its way, only slightly altered, into Springsteen's "Nebraska."

Springsteen's reaction to the book was surprising. As if no time had passed since the murders of a quarter century earlier, he called KMTV in Omaha, looking for Ninette Beaver. When I asked Springsteen what had motivated his effort to make contact with her, he seemed somewhat surprised at his own compulsion. "Really, I was up to something besides songwriting," Springsteen said. "I'm not sure what I thought I was doing. The book was pretty obvious. That was just . . . you could call it research. But the phone call was an unexpected thing for me to make. I'm not sure what led me to do that. But I was getting deeply into it, right?"

Equally surprising was the fact that Ninette Beaver was still working at the station when Springsteen called. And she was actually in the KMTV offices, not entirely sure who this was on the phone claiming to be Bruce Springsteen. By the time of *Caril's* 1974 publication, Fugate had been imprisoned since Starkweather's 1959 death by the electric chair. The KMTV reporter had stayed in touch with the "girl" as she entered adulthood in prison, as she found a way to live there, and, later, when she was released and attempted, with limited success, to find a life beyond the reach of her infamy. But as Beaver realized, Fugate's childhood experiences, no matter how far she got from a prison cell, were locked inside her, ticking. Springsteen understood that.

"At some point I said to myself that if I'm going to write a song about this," Springsteen told me, "there's something I need to get right. That song was going to be the entry point to the entire rest of the record. I sensed it. 'Nebraska' was one of the earliest ones. And I knew I was into a different style of songwriting at that time." He continued:

The song was one of those things that just feel central, and you sort of process the rest of your creative impulses through it at that given moment. That piece of music was the key in that moment. So, yeah, I knew I was into a different type of songwriting, one that—there were connections to Woody Guthrie in it, in some of the narrative, some of the detail—but it wasn't exactly something I'd heard before. It was a thing that I was just sussing out on my own, just feeling it all out. But when I made that phone call, I don't know. It was all just information, as far as I can understand. I've written plenty of music over the years that I've just flat out researched, to get the detail right. That's a part of the kind of writing that I do. It sort of began with that in some ways, but I think there was more going on. I don't remember doing it for any other songs on that record.

"Nebraska" anchored the record as a whole in violence and youth and the prison of image. And when Springsteen shifted the song to a first-person point of view, he was conjuring his own youth, in particular his grandparents' living room, there at 87 Randolph Street in Freehold.

CHAPTER TEN

87 Randolph Street

This is a backwater—you must be aware of that already.
Leaving here is like waking from a trance.

—MARILYNNE ROBINSON, *Gilead*

S hortly after the birth of his sister Virginia in 1951, Springsteen's family moved in with his paternal grandparents.
They would stay there through 1956, but the years spent in
that house would remain with Springsteen, a thing to untangle.
It was a period of his childhood that, in his telling, would come
to the fore in *Nebraska*.

"I know the house was very dilapidated," Springsteen told
me. "That was something that embarrassed me as a child. It was
visibly ramshackle, my grandparents' house. On the street you
could see that it was deteriorating. I just remember being embarrassed about it as a child. That would have been my only
sense that something wasn't right with who we were and what
we were doing. I can't quite describe it. It was intense. The
house was eventually condemned. Really, it fell apart around

us. I lived there when there was only one functional room, the living room. Everything else was pretty much finished."

In the living room was the portrait of his aunt Virginia, his father's sister, an image Springsteen has described on a few occasions. Virginia, at age six and out riding her bicycle, was hit and killed by a truck as it pulled out of a gas station on Freehold's McLean Street. In some misguided tribute to Virginia's early and sudden death, Springsteen's grandparents withheld discipline from their first grandchild, Bruce. It was a twisting of logic that likely seemed beneficent, if only to minds stuck in grief. His was a terrible freedom. When Bruce pushed, there was nothing there to push against.

WZ: I heard a term, "trans-generational haunting," that suggests the trauma from one generation can pass not just to the next generation but even skip over to the generation after that.

SPRINGSTEEN: Yeah, I believe that's true.

WZ: The way your grandparents lived out the loss of their daughter, your aunt, it was like they froze time. Did this mean trouble for the next generations?

SPRINGSTEEN: It was a lot of trouble for me. A lot of trouble for me was caused by that right there. Because I was the first child that came along after she died. So, I was my grandmother's charge. My mother was for some reason not big about motherhood at the time. So she kind of ceded me to my grandparents for the first six years of my life. That was . . . that was that.

WZ: In your book you describe your childhood experience as something like "His Majesty, the Baby."

SPRINGSTEEN: Oh yeah, that was me. Which seems to a kid like a great thing, but it's exactly what a kid doesn't want. Very problematic, and it caused me a lot of trouble. To this day. It destroyed me and it made me. At the same time.

This was the childhood to which Springsteen had returned as the songs for *Nebraska* spilled forth. When I asked him about the portrait of his aunt Virginia, he moved forward in his chair. "I have that," he said. "The one thing I have from that house is the picture of my aunt Virginia. It might be worth a look at. It was the center of the entire house. There in the middle of the living room wall. It was just always right over the top of the television. Her death was the essential event that defined the emotional life of that entire house. So that was a very . . . I'll go get it."

I didn't wait long before he came back. He set the portrait on the chair between us. I was on the couch, Springsteen was across from me in a chair, and the third point in our triangle was the image of Virginia, which otherwise hangs in Springsteen's writing room. When he was a boy, it had functioned as a shrine. It said, "We will *not* forget this loss." And in some ways the portrait fulfilled that function. Perhaps too well, because some part of Springsteen was, at the time of *Nebraska*'s writing, still back there, still captive to the theater of grief that gave his grandparents' crumbling house its identity. Returning again, through the songs, was nothing if not an attempted rescue mission, a man trying to find and save some part of himself.

The child's perspective is threaded throughout *Nebraska* and central in "Mansion on the Hill," "Used Cars," and "My Father's House." It's a point of view stripped of sentimentality, raw, almost undecided in its emotion. If the exact historical moment of *Nebraska* is uncertain, or at least shifting—the mention of the Philadelphia mobster Philip Testa, the Chicken Man in "Atlantic City," and the closing of the Mahwah auto plant in "Johnny 99" mark the period as the early 1980s, while "Open All Night" includes a Cobra Jet that could be from 1968 or a few years after—much of the record is, as Springsteen describes it, rooted in the time of his childhood, a black-and-white 1950s.

Like Starkweather, Springsteen experienced a period of living beyond consequences—however dramatically different the details. No one shaped his daily life through appropriate discipline. He could stay up as late as he wanted, watch television as the others slept. "There were no rules," he told the biographer Peter Ames Carlin, "I was living life like I've never heard of another child living it, to be honest with you." In *Born to Run* he describes his young self as a "tyrant," eating what he wanted when he wanted, a boy who "felt the rules were for the rest of the world." The discipline would come too late, in another household, his parents', after the family moved from Randolph Street in 1956 and when the struggles between father and son, as much as rock and roll, would begin to define the next period in his life. But when Springsteen says that the unchecked freedom in his grandparents' home shaped him, therein lies the key to his identification with an outsider experience as extreme as Charles Starkweather's:

> *Badlands* was *very* influential. I saw something I felt I knew in there, in that film. The life that I write about in *Nebraska*

is the life I was leading with my grandparents when we all lived in their house. It had a kerosene stove to heat the whole place, a coal stove to cook on in the kitchen, very old-school Irish. That was my grandparents, really old world. Even for our street, it was more backwards there. Our little house wasn't the same as the others. But it's their story in *Nebraska*. Much more the grandparents than my parents. I often go back to that house in my dreams, and it's still a place that holds a lot of significance for me, a lot of emotion. I pass by it a lot, still. It's a very mysterious place. I see it in a certain kind of light.

Springsteen's ambivalence about the world he came into and came from is spread across the songs of *Nebraska:* in the tension between familial allegiance and the law that underpins "Highway Patrolman," in the question of suffering's purpose in "Reason to Believe," in the paternal loss that can't finally be processed in "My Father's House." The years he lived at his grandparents' home had, as he says, destroyed him and had made him—so how does one, as an adult, reconcile those two extremes? The songs themselves are marked by the absence of easy answers, an absence of redemption, an absence of hope.

As the songwriting progressed, quickly and without the conscious shaping of themes and directions, there were a few songs that seemed not to belong to the bulk of material that was emerging, including "Pink Cadillac." Another, "Born in the U.S.A.," was written in that time but would later pull away from the pack, even if its original mood and feel gave it a place.

The songs arrived so fast and in such numbers that, in fact, there wasn't a lot of time to sit and ask questions of them.

"What are they and why are they here now? What is the thematic center?" Those would have been the right things to ask of the songs *if* Springsteen had thought he was making an album. But he didn't think he was making an album, just writing and preparing to throw down some rough recordings as reference. So there was no moment of pause to ask those questions of *any* of the songs . . . and he was too busy with the next one anyway.

Lines were repeated in a few different songs, though not as an artistic strategy. Springsteen just hadn't always finished the writing process. The singer-songwriter Chuck Prophet says he ultimately took that strange repetition of lines across songs as key information:

> We get some of those lyrics spilling over from "State
> Trooper" into "Open All Night"—"wee wee hours," "deliver me from nowhere"—like clues that these songs don't
> have the usual borders that separate one song from another.
> It's like this thing, *Nebraska*, just grew one night in a room
> in Colts Neck, New Jersey, the roots all tangled up, when
> this guy wrote these songs down instead of going to bed. It
> must've happened fast, so there was no laboring over even
> the morality of it all. In "Nebraska," Bruce gives this killer
> the voice in the song, kind of gets us on the side of this unrepentant criminal. There's more than a little moral ambiguity. I think that carries through a lot of *Nebraska*, that
> suspension of judgment. I believe Bruce cared about those
> people. It was almost like he was seeing how far his empathy, and ours, could extend. It would have been different, I

imagine, if he'd labored over the songs rather than just letting them come fast.

"It was the people in the songs," Scott Kempner says.

You never hate Johnny 99. You feel for him. They take his house away, he gets drunk, he kills somebody. You still don't hate him. He's all instinct. Nothing else in there but pure instinct. We all know a little about that, even if something finally keeps us in check. We see ourselves in there, and it really is seeing. All these songs on *Nebraska* are so cinematic. Really clear images, right from the first few songs, "Nebraska," "Atlantic City," "Mansion on the Hill," then, later, "Highway Patrolman." When you heard them, you saw them, and they didn't let you go. For all the music being made by major artists at that time, there was just nothing like *Nebraska*. It got us close to something about ourselves that we were not accustomed to talking about.

Patty Griffin, who covered *The River*'s "Stolen Car" on her *1000 Kisses* album, was struck by the violence that runs through the songs:

I think when I was in my thirties and digging into *Nebraska,* I was really just in awe of the storytelling. I wasn't listening for a big picture. It hit me over the head more recently, though, pulling it out and really listening to it again. It's just violence, violence, violence all through it. Different kinds of violences. About half of *Nebraska*'s songs are about people reacting to this thing that's destroying them by trying to destroy something else. It's a rare, rare thing to come across a record like that, any kind of work like that. And it's so well done. He paints his masterpiece of America as a brand and what it does to people. To me, *Nebraska* is an album-length description of how America has struggled to find its soul, has never had much of an identity beyond the brand that's been sold over and over again to people living here. But lives are lived behind the brand, and Springsteen is unearthing them, exposing them to the light.

The violence he portrayed, the refusal to judge his characters, the interest in rural scenes and outsiders: it was all a reflection of another key influence on *Nebraska,* the one that arguably matters almost as much as Malick's *Badlands,* the short stories of Flannery O'Connor.

Springsteen would eventually speak of the connection between *Nebraska* and O'Connor's writing, describing himself as being "deep into O'Connor" just before writing the *Nebraska* material. He'd discovered her work when Barbara Downey, his manager Jon Landau's wife, gave him a copy of O'Connor's collected stories. "My wife and I had a summer place in the '80s," says Landau, "and Bruce came out to visit. My wife had been reading Flannery O'Connor, and she thought Bruce might like it. So she gave him a copy of the short stories, which he still references to this day. With Bruce, you don't know what's going to stick, where it's going to come from, or what it's going to influence, often because his eyes are going to focus on something other eyes are not."

Writer Toby D'Anna describes Flannery O'Connor's short stories as shining "lights in moments of incredible darkness." O'Connor became known for coaxing something monumental from the stillness of American life. Remarking on her own living situation in Georgia, she said, "Lives spent between the house and the chicken yard do not make exciting copy." Nonetheless, that's where she went to work as a writer. A devout Catholic, she found in the stillness a violence and a stupidness, a "meanness," to borrow a word that resonated for Springsteen, that O'Connor's critics would have to reconcile, often clumsily, with her Catholic faith.

How could a believer such as O'Connor see the world as she portrayed it in "A Good Man Is Hard to Find," "Good Country People," "The Life You Save May Be Your Own"? "To the hard of hearing you shout," O'Connor explained, "and for the almost-blind you draw large and startling figures." Grotesques, really. "The characters are not 'likeable,'" Joseph O'Neil writes in *The Atlantic*, "but my God they are alive." The very same thing could be said of characters one finds in *Nebraska*.

In a 1998 conversation with Will Percy, nephew of the novelist Walker Percy, Springsteen spoke further of Flannery O'Connor:

> The really important reading that I did began in my late twenties, with authors like Flannery O'Connor. There was something in those stories of hers that I felt captured a certain part of the American character that I was interested in writing about. They were a big, big revelation. She got to the heart of some part of meanness that she never spelled

out, because if she spelled it out you wouldn't be getting it. It was always at the core of every one of her stories—the way that she'd left that hole there, that hole that's inside of everybody. There was some dark thing—a component of spirituality—that I sensed in her stories, and that set me off exploring characters of my own.

O'Connor's stories didn't hinge on redemption. Among her most lasting images is that of the traveling salesman's Bible in the story "Good Country People," a book hollowed out and containing a bottle of booze, some condoms, and a deck of cards with naked women on them. Just when you think it's one thing, the Good Book, it becomes another. The grandmother in "A Good Man Is Hard to Find" comes into her moment of grace, a word O'Connor liked, only as the killer on the loose, the Misfit, holds a gun in her face. In that instant, late in the story, she sees his humanity as it's bound up with her own . . . and then she's dead. " 'She would of been a good woman,' The Misfit said, 'if it had been somebody there to shoot her every minute of her life.'" In Flannery O'Connor's words, she was after those moments when she could reveal "the action of grace in territory held largely by the devil."

Until *Nebraska,* one got the sense that redemption was almost structural to the songs of Bruce Springsteen. "Thunder Road," "The River," "Racing in the Street." The redemption didn't always come easy, was sometimes only implied, but it came often, as some measure of hope, something to live for, an outline of possibility, sometimes delivered not just through words but through the music itself. But with *Nebraska* it's gone.

Flannery O'Connor trusted that her readers could see in her grotesques something more. Her fiction, and her Catholicism, hinged on that. Though Springsteen didn't work with what could be called grotesques, he did create characters caught in their own blocks of stone. *Nebraska* closes on "Reason to Believe," which might be summarized thus: there isn't one. "It's a common misinterpretation of 'Reason to Believe,' that it's a hopeful song," Springsteen told me. "It's hard to find a basis for that misinterpretation. I suppose the title does it. But it was one of the darkest songs on the record and it was the way I decided to finish that album. In that density." It might have been O'Connor who let Springsteen know that he could end right there and his listeners would, hopefully, know what to do with it.

———

When Springsteen's pile of songs accumulated, his mind went not to understanding the material he'd gathered but to capturing it on tape. Understanding could come later—for those who would discover the songs, and for Springsteen himself. With pages of lyrics gathered in a notebook, lines crossed out and rewritten, sometimes incomplete, Springsteen then did something he'd never done, setting up that makeshift studio at home so that he could record demos of the songs. It didn't matter that he was moving too fast to get to know them. Songs, unlike people, have remarkable patience as they wait for someone to hear what they're saying.

CHAPTER ELEVEN

Darkness on the Edge of Bed

The TEAC Model 144 Portastudio brings top-quality
creative recording capabilities within the reach of the home
studio enthusiast and serious musician/engineer—with
unprecedented economy and portability.

—from the TEAC 144 user's manual

L aughing, Springsteen described the Colts Neck recording room as "lightly furnished." It was his bedroom. When I asked why, with other rooms available, he would record in the bedroom, he hesitated, as if he hadn't stopped to consider that. "You know, I lived there by myself and it was a relatively small house. I'm sure there was a guest bedroom somewhere, but this was just where I was comfortable. I'm sitting on the end of my bed and singing and playing. It was beyond casual. I put the mic up there. And this was where I'd usually sit and sing, the end of my bed." The microphone he was singing into was connected to a TEAC 144 four-track recorder.

He'd sent his roadie, Mike Batlan, to pick up a machine he could use at home to make demos. Batlan grabbed a TEAC 144 at what the manufacturer would later describe as nothing more than a "local music store." Coupling that with a few Shure SM57 microphones, affordable, workhorse microphones, Springsteen had his home studio. Batlan looked at the 144's manual, apparently not for long, and got Springsteen far enough that the songwriter could begin cutting tracks and doing the few overdubs the 144 would allow. The multitracking capacity of the machine would allow Springsteen to layer some musical elements over his basic voice-and-guitar tracks. He could, if he chose, even create the sound of a small combo, but that wasn't what he was after. It would be the sound of one man.

The arrival of the TEAC 144, priced at $899 retail, meant multitrack recording could be done on a cassette. It was still a new technology, a novelty. You could buy your recording tape at a convenience store, ten good cassettes for twenty bucks or so. To increase the quality of the recording, TEAC doubled the tape speed from that of a normal consumer cassette recorder, from 1⅞ inches per second (ips) to 3¾ ips.

Professional recording machines, the kind Springsteen had used when making albums, were a different matter altogether. One reel of tape cost around fifty dollars, and if it had been put in casing like a cassette, it would have been about as thick as a standard dictionary. Those professional machines sent the tape over the recording heads at a speed almost ten times faster than the TEAC 144. More tape over the recording heads meant better quality. All that said, the TEAC 144 was still the first major bid to establish a territory between studio-grade recording gear and the cassette recorders that kids played with.

The revolution of the four-track cassette recorder really was this: multitrack recording could be done at home. If in the moment it was a quiet development, it was nonetheless a landmark in the larger story of recording. The user's manual for the TEAC 144 made it sound, well, better than it was. "Top quality recording capabilities," the manual promised, for the "serious musician/engineer." It was a promise made by people with a product to sell. The 144 was not a machine for musicians looking to make hit records. At most, for that class of artist it was a tool. The cassette technology situated the machine in the world of the consumer and, beyond that, the musician's "work tape."

The Maxell cassettes Springsteen pushed into the 144 were the same ones he'd use when he recorded rehearsals with the E Street Band. "Cassette players were extremely important for us," recalled Steven Van Zandt. "We'd put a cassette recorder in the middle of rehearsal to tape it. In those days, for a certain amount of time, there was a self-limiter on the microphone, so it wouldn't distort. You could play as a full rock band, full volume, and it would sound incredible—on a cassette player." It was the sound Keith Richards and Charlie Watts got on "Street Fighting Man," recorded in a hotel room on a cheap Philips recorder, the kind that could be picked up at a London department store.

"We'd go into the recording studio," Van Zandt continued, "and we'd have to try to get *this* sound, the one we got on a twenty-dollar cassette recorder. So it was a major part of everybody's life in those days. Because that's how you recorded your rehearsals or ideas you had for songs. You can't beat that sound. It's just a fantastic sound." The cheap devices using cassette tape had a special quality, the warmth of magnetic tape, the rich sound of tape saturation, all colored by built-in limiting/compression. What Van Zandt describes, however, was not multitrack recording. It was one-track, mono recording put down on a cassette, the tape width roughly one-eighth of an inch as opposed to the two inches for professional tape. But when Springsteen got the TEAC 144 going, which *was* a multitrack machine, he was ripping the plastic off a fresh Maxell and thinking of the loose, on-the-fly world of rehearsals and work tapes, not of commercial recordings intended for release.

"Bruce had gotten this four-track cassette player," recalled Van Zandt, laughing. "Which was highly evolved technologically from our usual mono, one-track. And I guess, I don't know, he was doing demos for what would become *Born in the U.S.A.,* eventually. And he just did them with his roadie, his guitar roadie, working the dials and keeping it from distorting or whatever. And he did a bunch of these things." The guy known for laboring over *Born to Run, Darkness on the Edge of Town, The River,* a legend in second-guessing himself and perfectionism, wasn't getting in his own way. Because he didn't know he was making an album.

> SPRINGSTEEN: I mean it wasn't produced. I don't know if there's even a recording credit. I don't think there's any engineering credit.
>
> WZ: Mike Batlan got a recording credit.
>
> SPRINGSTEEN: Did he? Damn, that's good. It was just an undone record. None of those skills came into play. Consciously into play, let's say. They were unmanned positions.

In the first few years that followed the TEAC 144's introduction, it was common enough to hear people, particularly the aspirational types who had just picked up their new 144s, say,

"The Beatles made *Sgt. Pepper's* on a four-track." While true, the Beatles sure as hell weren't using a TEAC 144. The four-track machines at Abbey Road, which to this day remain coveted by artists and producers, were studio grade, using one-inch tape and operating at significantly higher tape speeds than the 144. The microphones used were of equal quality, no comparison with the Shure 57s Springsteen was using. And by *Sgt. Pepper's* the Beatles were syncing two machines together in order to have more tracks. No one should have felt disappointed that their 144 demos didn't sound like "Fixing a Hole."

What the 144 user's manual didn't say, because the makers of the machine didn't know this nor did anyone else at the time, was that the TEAC 144 would mark the beginning of a home-recording revolution that would, eventually, prove a significant threat to commercial studios. While being an analog, tape-based machine, the TEAC 144 was a step toward a digital age when multitrack recording of a much higher quality could be done on most laptops, not to mention what could be achieved with the various stand-alone units and software programs that would become available for home use.

By the start of the twenty-first century, artists wouldn't need the commercial studios to nearly the same degree that they had in prior decades. People could and would make hit records at home on a regular basis. But, in terms of quality, an early device like the TEAC 144 was still far closer to that twenty-dollar cassette recorder than it was to the equipment at costly studios like the Hit Factory and the Power Station.

Toby Scott would work on Springsteen projects from 1978 through 2017, often exclusively. As an engineer, he had his own view of the effects on recorded music as artists began to do more and more recording in home studios. "The introduction of the home capability?" Scott asked pausing before answering his own question. "I was always like, 'This is not gonna be good.'"

> The TEAC 144 was just the beginning. What's happening now is that anyone can do it, make something with GarageBand. People can record at home. That drummer [Gary Mallaber] who played on *Lucky Town,* I saw him two weeks ago, and he'd gotten back from Nashville. He said, "It's changed! There's a few big studios, but everybody is working at home!" To a certain extent what's happening is that, yeah, everybody's recording at home, but the regular guy that has no recording instruction, who has no basis to understand what a recording could be, is acting as the engineer. So people record stuff like Bruce, and with the latest, digital version of something like his *Nebraska* technology.

But, of course, Springsteen wasn't making a record. "These songs had been in my head and on paper for a bit, still kind of evolving, even if they were sometimes close," Springsteen insisted. "The recordings, though, were just meant to get us a jump start on work in the studio with the band. I'd always spent a lot of time writing in the studio. I was trying to be more efficient, I guess. Certainly trying to spend a little less money."

Writing songs in a commercial recording studio is a little like storing your winter clothes in a room at the Four Seasons. It gets costly. Springsteen knew what it was like to be a rock and roll star carrying a lot of debt. Maybe he was getting too old for that. What works in your twenties doesn't always make the

same sense rounding the corner of the next decade. So he figured he'd work some stuff out at home, then finish it in the
studio, saving himself a nice sack of cash. "I certainly didn't
spend long recording it, you know? I was putting things down
only as a kind of reference."

Once Batlan set up the TEAC 144, Springsteen, unencum-
bered, got right to work. By most accounts, the night of January 3, 1982, was the session that captured the bulk of the
Nebraska recordings. Batlan was there and not there. "He gave
me a gift of helping without being a presence, was kind of invisible," Springsteen recalled. "I felt alone, and I needed that for
these songs."

As far as instruments went, the leading role in the making of
Nebraska was played by Springsteen's acoustic guitar. "A J-200,
a Gibson," he told me, asking me to wait where I was while he
went to get it. Back moments later with the guitar in hand, he
showed me the instrument, letting the afternoon sun play across
its surface as only a guitar player can do, before setting it down
in its own seat, next to the portrait of his aunt Virginia. "I believe this, too, was a gift from Mike Batlan," he told me.

The Gibson J-200 is a guitar that has some stories of its own
and brought the right kind of past to *Nebraska*. It's the model
Ike Everly played around the time his sons, Phil and Don, were
teenagers in Ike's family band, a radio act. The boys learned to
love the J-200, later getting their own, and finally, from Gibson, the smaller-bodied versions that would be their signature
Everly Brothers guitars. Elvis and Neil Diamond, George Har-
rison and Jimmy Page, Emmylou Harris, all have had J-200s
within reach.

The electric guitar used on the album was the *Born to Run*

guitar, a mongrel, with parts from a Fender Telecaster and a Fender Esquire, both of a 1950s vintage. "It had to have been the Tele," Springsteen told me. But he doesn't think there was an amplifier in the room. "My recollection is it was straight into the TEAC. I think I maybe had an acoustic twelve string there. Yeah. And I guess I had a little mandolin somewhere. Harmonicas, of course. And then the glockenspiel. Most necessary," Springsteen said to me, laughing.

But the glockenspiel *was* most necessary. "I wanted that sound because it harked back to childhood, gave a sense of coming from that childlike space," Springsteen explained to me. "I don't remember if there's glockenspiel used in Terrence Malick's *Badlands,* but if there's not, there's *something* in the instrument that reminds me of what's used on the film's soundtrack. That had something to do with me wanting the glockenspiel on 'Nebraska' and, I think, a few other songs. As I've said, I was kind of looking for . . . some of the songs were coming from that Charles Laughton, *The Night of the Hunter* aesthetic, a really dark twisted childhood fairy tale or folktale. That had a lot to do with why I wanted that glockenspiel sound."

True to Springsteen's recollection, the *Badlands* score weaves Orff instruments throughout, the xylophones, marimbas, and glockenspiels associated with Orff Schulwerk, a method and instrumentation for early childhood music education invented by the German composer Carl Orff. It was a sound that, for Springsteen, evoked both melancholy and a hint of menace. "There's a bringing forth of the darkness of the natural world," Springsteen told me. "If you watch *The Night of the Hunter* and see how it's filmed, it's a lot of images of the woods and shots like the classic close-up of the rabbit. Terrence Malick picks up on that in all his films, where the natural world plays such a big part, that meditative, that *deadly* meditative feeling of nature. It brings forth a sort of mythic dread. It's inherent in all the characters on *Nebraska*."

So the TEAC 144 was on a table. The two Shure 57 microphones were on mic stands, one for vocals/harmonica and the other for the Gibson J-200. There were a few extra cables and some pens and notebooks. The glockenspiel and the other percussion instruments were things lying around the house. Then it was just a matter of pressing play and record at the same time. Mistakes had to be egregious to stop the process. If a take felt lacking, he'd just do another, keeping them both. There wasn't a lot of listening back, mostly just moving ahead. The overdubs, though they were limited, were done in the same kind of loose spirit. Springsteen was thinking more about songs than recordings.

————

For songwriters and record makers of Springsteen's analog generation, a psychological divide often separated the recording of demos from the recording of albums intended for release. Demo recording had little to none of the pressure of album making. In typical commercial recording studios, a red light would go on when recording was taking place. Singers in particular were known for losing themselves in the presence of those red lights. It was as if there were an ambulance in the room. Some singers thrive at an accident scene; many don't.

Those singers in commercial studios were also regularly isolated from everyone else, on the other side of some thick glass, in a kind of performance aquarium. The idea was to deliver the best vocal possible, often with a group of people listening and watching from a control room, all prepared to pass judgment on a take, sometimes regardless of their qualifications (thus the great struggle to keep label executives out of recording studios).

A sensitive engineer in a commercial studio could light some candles, provide bourbon, maybe put up a poster of Brigitte Bardot, or give the rest of the band money to go play miniature golf, just to get them out of there while the singer pushed out a vocal track, but the heightened self-consciousness of a "final" studio performance often remained. Cutting demos was far closer to the looseness of live performance. Closer still to singing in the shower. You knew it wasn't for an audience. Being naked makes sense there. In those ways and others, commercial studios offered a marked contrast to the home demo environment, the end-of-the-bed world where Springsteen cut *Nebraska*.

At home with his TEAC 144, Springsteen was just knocking songs off, making rough sketches, no one looking over his shoulder. He felt free, certainly not self-conscious, not under any kind of scrutiny. His goals were modest. The only things he might waste there in Colts Neck were a few bucks on cassette tapes and his own time. He was at liberty to explore the worlds of the songs rather than analyze his performances. His voice was different, not needing to fight its way through the sound of a band.

It was probably beginning to strike Springsteen as the recordings started to accumulate that the bulk of the material had certain family traits, in mood, character, and musical feel. Mostly, the songs seemed to connect, asserting themselves as a collection. Springsteen had written some pretty dark songs along the way. "Hungry Heart" was like a study in human trouble, with only a few short verses, but, no matter the song's content, as a pop production it got Springsteen his first top ten single and sent a clear message to the dance floor. It certainly isn't the case that people can only shimmy to happy songs. But the *Nebraska* material was different. Or Springsteen was. Or both.

Once the recordings were done—even if they were just demos—they needed to be mixed down from the TEAC 144 to a standard cassette so that the music could be played back on any consumer device, in a car, on a stereo, wherever. Springsteen would need to mix them down to be able to share them with Jon Landau, with the E Street Band. In the midst of that process Springsteen would, for the first time, hear the songs outside the experience of writing and performing them, *as a listener.* The mixing process was, of course, as casual as the rest of the recording, free from second-guessing. Needing a cassette player to mix onto, Springsteen and Mike Batlan used Springsteen's Panasonic boom box, which was water damaged and had only recently started working again.

Springsteen had been canoeing on the Navesink River with Garry Tallent one afternoon when the boom box got hit with water over the bow. It seemed to destroy the thing. Springsteen didn't throw the machine out, though, and instead left it sitting on his couch, no proper burial. Bachelor style. Then, weeks later and very suddenly, while Springsteen was by himself and watching late-night television, it came back to life, playing whatever cassette had been left in it. It's a telling detail as far as revealing his ambitions for those home recordings. You don't master your recordings to a water-damaged Panasonic boom box if you're looking to follow up *The River.*

But not only did Springsteen use the Panasonic for mix-down; he also, in the mix process, put all the recordings through a Gibson Echoplex, which put a layer of early Sun Records–style slap echo on, well, everything: vocals, guitars, harmonica, percussion, glockenspiel. As decisions go, to mix every recorded track on a multitrack recording through a single effect is certainly not the kind of choice professional engineers tended to make when they were creating recordings for commercial release. But Springsteen wasn't thinking like a professional engineer. He just wanted a reference for the "real" recording process, something the band could listen to before they made a final version.

"Yeah, everything went through the Echoplex," he told me, laughing. "Guitar, voice, everything. It all has that weird echo." When I said to Springsteen that I felt it ended up being a crucial part of the recording's character, he stopped laughing and nodded, agreeing that it was exactly right for the recordings, even if it was foolhardy. "It *was* the right thing," he said. "I have good instincts. I've always had good instincts. Sit me down in front of the elements, and I'll put them together in a way that makes the most aesthetic sense. So that's basically what happened with whatever you want to call it, the mixing process of that record. It was very . . . everything was done in five minutes. The sound I was looking for, we found it through the Echoplex and that beatbox."

Much as the glockenspiel evoked a certain strain of childhood trouble, the anxious woods of the fairy-tale world, the Echoplex called to mind the sound of Elvis's early recordings. It transported the whole operation to a particular elsewhere. Springsteen elaborated:

It's interesting, you know? Why are the Sun sessions Elvis's best? It's the spontaneity. That short echo. They've got a little *Nebraska* in them. Those records, they're pretty closely connected in some strange metaphysical way. I suppose their relationship would be in the characters but also, without a doubt, in the sound. It's a dissociative sound. It's the sound of distance. It's the sound of the past, of history, in some way. It just brings all of that with it. When you really put slap on something, that particular echo, you're altering time and space. The echo effects were essential to *Nebraska,* which is one of the first things we messed up when we went to try and make it better. You're not going to mix a whole record through an Echoplex when you're doing a proper mix in a studio. But even the kind of echo found in a professional recording studio was too clean. Once again, we were gifted by our gear and the equipment that we were casually using at that moment.

The tape that came out of the boom-box mixdown had another unexpected quality, arrived at inadvertently: when taken to another cassette player and played back, it would play at a slower speed. The boom box might have been working, but it wasn't working perfectly. It was running fast, which meant that when the mixdown cassette was played on any other device, everything would be slowed *down* slightly, putting Springsteen's voice and music under another layer of gray. At first, no one even noticed. But the mood deepened.

The cassette would go first to his manager, Jon Landau. Landau was a very different collaborator, in style and temperament, from anyone else in Springsteen's world. By that time in their relationship, when the recordings and an attached note got to Landau, the manager and the artist were deep into one of the great partnerships in American music, a collaboration that began in 1974 and continues today. Landau's reaction to the new recordings was immediate and unambiguous. He was, Dave Marsh writes, "taken aback at the dark tenor of so much of the material." The tape, Landau told me, "concerned [him] on a friendship level." Landau heard something, an anxious quality, that no one else would in the early stages of the project. His concern would prove justified.

CHAPTER TWELVE

How About We Stop This?

WZ: How would you describe what wasn't working when you went to rerecord?

SPRINGSTEEN: Every step I took in trying to make it better, I lost my people.

WZ: As though the characters of *Nebraska* had 51 percent of the vote? Like they were going to say what this album was going to be?

SPRINGSTEEN: That's always the case, if you're doing it right.

WZ: But these characters in particular were way out on the margins of life. These characters had a sound of their own.

SPRINGSTEEN: Yes. And so my job was simply to recognize that and not fuck it up.

A mere three weeks or so after that January 3 Colts Neck session, and before Jon Landau got the tape of the home mixes, the E Street Band was at the Power Station working on a different project, recording "Cover Me," a song Springsteen was readying for Donna Summer. Landau, in the control room listening back to the basic tracks of "Cover Me," felt validated in his initial sense about the song, which came to him almost as soon as the band started working it out there at the studio: "Cover Me" was too good to give away. He'd lost arguments of this kind on several occasions, but that didn't stop him trying again. During the recording of *Darkness on the Edge of Town,* both Patti Smith's recording of "Because the Night" and the Pointer Sisters' of "Fire" landed high on the charts as Landau, Springsteen, and the E Street Band struggled to complete their own project. For Landau, it was at times a source of frustration:

> I think one reason why he never finished "Because the Night" and instead gave it to Patti Smith was that it was similar to "Fire"—if it had been on the album it would have been *the* song, the first thing everyone would gravitate to. The Pointer Sisters' "Fire" went to number two. Then "Because the Night" goes top ten! So both of those hits happen while we're still making *Darkness*. But Bruce was so rigorous in his view of albums as albums, he was protective of them. And big singles could affect that.

The legendary engineer, mixer, and producer Bob Clearmountain, who would mix many of Springsteen's recordings, recalls another, later installment in that same general story. It was the first session for *The River*, which produced "Roulette." New to the Springsteen team and unaware of the dynamics, Clearmountain was struck by what they'd recorded. After a playback of "Roulette," he looked at Springsteen and said, "This sounds like a single." Behind Springsteen's back was Landau, making silent hand gestures to Clearmountain that said, "No! No, don't say that!" Clearmountain didn't know what was going on. Only later did he realize that, for the first time, he'd met an artist capable of worrying that they might be cutting a hit single.

In the session that produced "Cover Me," Landau, feeling sure that Springsteen was ready to make an album that could build on and exceed the success of *The River*, lobbied to keep

HOW ABOUT WE STOP THIS? | 163

"Cover Me" for the next album. That album had no name, of course. At that point it had nothing but the song "Cover Me," if Landau even had a chance of winning the argument.

But, for once, Landau got his way. Springsteen would give Donna Summer and her then producer, Quincy Jones, another song, "Protection." "Cover Me" thus took its place as the first recorded track for Bruce Springsteen's next release. In Landau's view, it was a promising start to the creation of what he hoped would be the big record he knew his artist had in him and deserved. Next he just needed to hear what else Springsteen had been writing. If "Cover Me" was any sign, this was going to be all that Landau was hoping for. But shortly after recording "Cover Me," Landau received the Colts Neck tapes, with a handwritten note attached.

Springsteen's note to Landau:

There is all sorts of stuff here. What I did is put anything on I thought would be good for you to hear. I still left off about 5 to 7 things that I hadn't finished or really wanted the band to work out with. Many of the songs may need editing, lines changed, arrangements changed. Some will really work, others may just need to be put aside but there was something in each one I got a kick out of so it's included. I got a lot of ideas but I'm not exactly sure of where I'm going. I guess the only thing I looked for in the songs was that it somehow break a little new ground for me. They all don't do this some I just got a blast out of but I think a good amount do or at least try. [At that point he draws a stick figure with a guitar that says, "Let's Rock!"]

They may not hit you right away, or they may sound a little foreign. They were mostly all written—except Bye Bye Johnny—from the time we got off tour to right before Christmas, about 3½ months. So here it is!

1) <u>Bye Bye Johnny</u>—No explanation necessary
2) <u>Starkweather</u> or <u>Nebraska</u>—4 mixes
   #1 with 12 string—complete version. This song may need editing or verses switched but it might be right as it is. This is about the Charles Starkweather murder spree in Nebraska in the 50's. Mix #2 early fade. #3 Bad harp no good. #4 with glock.
3) <u>Atlantic City</u>—3 different takes—all with slightly different arrangement and lyric changes. #1 Take 1. #2 Take 3. #3 Take 4. This song should probably be done with whole band and really rockin' out.
   SKIP—This song comes #6 on the tape—<u>Johnny 99</u>—2 versions, kinda fun! These words are not completely worked out or finished and so the singing is occasionally awkward. I don't know if this song is a keeper or not but I thought you'd get a kick out of it. #1 Take 2. #2 Take 3 different end verse.
4) <u>Mansion on the Hill</u>—3 mixes.
   and with slight balance change / first two mixes are a little dirty. 3rd is best recording quality.
5) <u>Born in the U.S.A.</u>—you sent me the Paul Schrader script which I did not have the chance to read yet but I did whip up this little ditty purloining it's [sic] title. On this number song should be done very hard rockin'.

This song is in very rough shape but it is as good as I can get it at the moment. It might have potential.

6) <u>Johnny 99</u>—see above

7) <u>Down Bound Train</u>—uptempo rocker for full effect needs band / could be exciting.

8) <u>Losin' Kind</u>—searched and searched for a better title. Spent many hours on this task but no good. I like the verses but I can't seem to find a better punch line. Kind of like a James M. Cain story. Could be done with more of a band arrangement. 3 Takes—all slight lyric changes (1st and last verse)

9) <u>State Trooper</u>—I dreamed this one up comin' back from New York one night. I don't know if it's really even a song or not but I did it so I figured I'd throw it on. It's kinda weird.

10) <u>Used Cars</u>—the exciting story of my own personal life. 2 takes. 1st is a little dirty recording wise. 2nd cleaner.

11) <u>Wanda (Open All Night)</u>—in which the hero braves snow sleat [sic] rain and the highway patrol for a kiss from his baby's lips. This song is very hard to perform. 2 takes. 2nd more voice.

12) <u>the Child Bride</u>—in which the protagonist violates the Mann Act and is left to ponder his fate. This is kind of a work in progress or more like without progress. I worked a real long time on this song and could never quite get it right. I spent so much time on it I thought I'd include it to see what you think.

13) <u>Pink Cadillac</u>—self explanatory.

14) <u>Highway Patrolman</u>—this is the same as "<u>Child Bride</u>"

and to a lesser degree "Losin' Kind." Worked very long
on this and always had the feeling I was coming up
short. Not really finished but is about as good as I can
get it at the time. Don't think the ending was quite
strong enough.

15) <u>Reason to Believe</u>—No not the Tim Hardin song but
a completely original tune by the same name culled
from my own experience driving down Highway 33
on my way to Millstone. 2 takes. Second has extra
verse.

As Springsteen explained to me, he'd never come to Landau
with a collection of songs on tape. In the past, he'd shared recently written material in the midst of recording sessions, or let
new ideas emerge in that same context, where Landau could
witness a song's birth. He remembered:

Jon was typically introduced to songs in the studio. So this
is the first time I ever sent him a collection of them on a
cassette. And I knew if I'm sending this stuff to Jon as my
next record, he needs a little preparation. He needs an introduction of some sort, whether it's humor, whatever, he
needs an entrance into it. I don't remember his initial reaction to the songs, but it might have been some puzzlement.
That's what I was kind of prepared for, you know? This
tape was something pretty different. But I don't remember
our initial conversations. I made the package, threw a funny
little note in, and sent it off. Because I knew myself that
what was in there was very good. I had some inner feeling,

some sense that something had happened that was going to
need to be reckoned with on some level. Right then I
didn't think that meant releasing it—I'm *not* releasing it—
but it has to be dealt with. It's some part of my talent that I
have to recognize and address.

Springsteen's note to Landau serves as a clue to the clueless-
ness of the moment. No matter the level at which Springsteen
was operating, firmly established as one of America's great
songwriters, that note tells us that Springsteen either wasn't
sure what he had or was worried that Landau might be, so his
written descriptions of the songs pull away from the hopelessness captured in the songs. The joking tone of the letter rubs
strangely against the tape's content.

Communications between Landau and Springsteen would
take different forms over the years. More recently, Landau remarked to me that Bruce loved to send text messages. In some
periods it was the telephone. But just then, with these songs
and in that technological window, it was a handwritten note
with some almost extemporaneous thoughts, delivered to Landau's office by a guy who drove in from Jersey. In that moment,
Springsteen didn't have a lot more to say about the songs because he didn't necessarily know a lot about them himself.

The cassette contained multiple mixes of several songs, and
the note described the variations among them. The combination of levity and uncertainty in the written message suggests a
songwriter in the middle of work, not done. For all the sense
of presentation, Springsteen's comments are shot through with
ambivalence, broad strokes, and misfires. You could have put

question marks after a number of his statements. "Highway Patrolman" he describes in the note as "coming up short," a song and recording that would later rank as one of his very best, exactly as it was.

Landau listened, shared a few thoughts, and returned the tape to Springsteen. It was the only copy, so Springsteen needed it back. Sessions were booked for April, again at the Power Station, and the truth was that until then Landau couldn't say a whole lot about the songs. The band needed to be there, playing the material, so Landau could hear them as they became fully realized recordings. The preliminary sketches on the tape couldn't tell him much about what the material would become as productions, recorded professionally.

When it came to working with Springsteen, Landau's experience of making records had often been one of expectations reversed, welcome accidents, failed efforts, unplanned victories. No one knows what's going to happen once recording begins. Like any other artistic enterprise, it's a process never fully in control of itself. The gods have the final word. A song could become a thousand different recordings. And just because a good song is written doesn't mean a good record will come of it. So, for the most part, Landau held his thoughts in reserve.

―――――――――

Come April, Springsteen returned to the Power Station, this time bringing the cassette as a reference for the sessions. He had it in his pocket, no case. There was lint on it. The E Street Band had assembled, and they worked with all the intention, energy, and expectation that album making requires. The trajectory of Springsteen's career was such that it would be foolish to do otherwise. On the second day of the sessions it became clear that the tape had a few different things to tell them.

The Power Station approach to "Born in the U.S.A." was a significant departure from the Colts Neck demo. Max Weinberg's snare took on a central role, due in part to a gated reverb. It wasn't just that, though; it was the way in which that snare got the gift of space. A repeated synthesizer line and Springsteen's vocal were the only competing elements. In the intro, the first verse, and the first chorus all three came to the fore while the rest of the band sat back.

In Springsteen's productions to date there was no precedent for what they were hearing in the control room speakers. This was not *The River*, with a full band jumping on a song at the four count. It was a snare sound that demanded the others stand back and wait. Later there would even be rumors that the drum was triggered, a sample. The music business has always generated plenty of rumors regarding human misconduct, but when there are rumors about a drum sound? That tells you something about the impact of a recording.

You could say that it was the first time the influence of the digital age could be heard in a Bruce Springsteen recording, whether it was an analog recording or not. A Linn LM-1 Drum Computer using digital samples had been introduced a few years earlier, doing its part to usher in an era when the snare drum could be isolated and brought up to new levels in a recording's mix. As a technological shift, it affected even those drummers still sitting at acoustic sets, playing to analog tape. The BBC's Neil Brand described the "Born in the U.S.A." drum and synth sounds as, taken together, something meant to "pummel the listener into submission." Jon Landau recalls:

> We had that drum sound on that record. Everybody wanted that sound for a while. Even to this day you rarely hear drums with just the sonic power they had. It was so electrifying when we recorded it. It's an experience that was unforgettable. I forget a lot of the details of the past, but not that. When that happened, every person in the room, whoever was there, the assistant engineer or anyone in the band, everybody in the room felt like, "This is as good as it gets." It was a milestone. We'd done something in this studio that hadn't been done before. With that song we'd captured some part of Bruce's thing that we hadn't up to that point. The greatness of the song wasn't revealed to me in the demo, wasn't something I heard until we were recording.

Roy Bittan played his synthesizer riff on a Yamaha CS-80, hardly a tool of the garage band, and it would come together with Max Weinberg's snare to give the song its anthemic character and sonic currency. Few would be talking about Woody Guthrie when Springsteen released "Born in the U.S.A." as a single. There was an energy that no one in the recording studio had planned on. Only a few takes in and the band had the recorded version of "Born in the U.S.A." that would eventually open the album of the same name. This is what Springsteen had wanted for all of the Colts Neck demos, to hit liftoff. But that's not what happened.

If you were working on the new Bruce Springsteen project at the Power Station during the April–May sessions that year you would have every reason to believe that things were going well. Even *very* well. For a songwriter with Springsteen's output, it seemed there would always be more songs than needed. Completing albums, for Springsteen, typically involved the hard decision of saying what songs would be included and what songs would be shelved. That certainly wasn't the case for all acts. So, with "Cover Me" done already and "Born in the U.S.A." arriving like an announcement that something bold and fresh and even daring was coming into being, who in the room was going to feel that things were not working? Only one person.

As Toby Scott describes it, the recording sessions went quickly after that. "Working on the Highway," a near-complete reworking of "Child Bride," and "Downbound Train" came from the Colts Neck sessions. Both worked as band recordings. They were added to "Cover Me" and "Born in the U.S.A." Four cuts—"Darlington County," "Glory Days," "I'm Goin' Down," and "I'm on Fire"—came next. They were not from the Colts Neck sessions but were drawn from material Springsteen had available, some written earlier, some more recently. That brought the total to eight. This meant that the lion's share of *Born in the U.S.A.* was ready to be mixed by the end of those three weeks at the Power Station.

Toby Scott's gut sense was that Springsteen was uncomfortable with how smoothly (read "quickly") the sessions were

going. It could have been a celebratory moment. Why not? It
was obviously a matter of perception. Scott saw it this way:

> The band went through, and after a period of experimen-
> tation as to how to play "Born in the U.S.A.," they came
> up with a way to do it. As I remember it, the entire band
> played the song at the same time. That was the take. When
> they heard this back, we all went, "Whew, this is kind of a
> *sound*." I didn't know if this was what Bruce had in mind,
> but, boy, everybody liked it, obviously. So we went on.
> Zipped through the recording. At least a song a day for a
> couple weeks. Then we did overdubs, then from studio A
> up to the C room to mix. I started mixing, and then Bruce
> was like, "Wow." I think things were moving too fast for
> him. He tends to be very deliberate, likes to analyze stuff
> and make sure everything is how he wants it. And here we
> are, three or four weeks into the record, and we're mixing.
> He said, "How about we stop this?"

Sitting on top of two-thirds of *Born in the U.S.A.*, including
five recordings that would become top ten singles, Springsteen
was somewhere else. The record that was going to change his
public life, that would make him one of the biggest stars in the
history of popular music, was, in three short weeks, taking
shape. But the record that was going to change his private life,
his inner life, was the one that interested him, the one that
compelled him, that woke him at 3:00 a.m.

Jon Landau remembers the ambivalence Springsteen felt at
the time:

Bruce kept doing this dance between accepting and embracing the album he was making that would have "Born in the U.S.A.," that would have "Glory Days," that would have "Cover Me," the song that he wrote for Donna Summer and didn't send it to her because I said please, please don't. I'd heard "Born in the U.S.A.," and I felt it was some kind of hit. I didn't know if it was a Top 40 hit, but I knew it was going to get people's attention. "Glory Days"? It felt like a smash. So he knew in my opinion that, on one hand, he was onto something that could be really explosive and raise his profile as a mass artist. He had reservations about that. No secret. And he'd written this collection of songs, the *Nebraska* material, that was very independent, certainly not geared toward mass appeal. Two extremes. Same songwriter. Same time. It's like he had his *Star Wars* and his art movie in his hand at the same moment. And he went to *Nebraska* first. It's just where he had to go.

At the Power Station, they had tried various approaches in their efforts to record "Nebraska," "Highway Patrolman," "Atlantic City," "Mansion on the Hill," and the other songs that would make up *Nebraska*. In Springsteen's original note to Landau, he described material like "Atlantic City" as something that could work "with whole band and really rockin' out." But after trying just that, Springsteen changed his opinion. Whether with the full band, with just Max Weinberg and Roy Bittan, even performing the songs alone, nothing seemed to capture the spirit of the cassette recordings. Perhaps the most troubling detail was that the songs weren't even working as recordings when Springsteen played them solo. There was no band overpowering the songs then, so where did the songs go? While "Born in the U.S.A." and "Downbound Train" rolled out with relative ease, the others—"Nebraska," "Highway Patrolman," "Atlantic City," "Reason to Believe," "Mansion on the Hill," "Used Cars," "Johnny 99," "State Trooper," and "Open All Night"— would not yield.

"It seemed pretty obvious pretty quickly," Landau recalled to me,

> that this was not falling into place very easily. Bruce wasn't coming in the control room after the takes and high-fiving everybody. It seemed like it wasn't working. Now, at that point in the process, you could ask, "Is this not working because these aren't the right songs?" Or you could say, "These are the right songs, but this is the wrong music— done with the band." If your view was, "We're making the next album, and these are the songs." Well, they're not coming out very well. But, again, you could look at it and say, "Look, are these even the right songs? Maybe we just need some more rock songs, you know?" But, as I said, the songs on the tape, most of them, resisted intervention. Bruce had put months into the writing, and something was there. But for a time we were unsure how to proceed.

Nebraska and *Born in the U.S.A.* were eventually going to look like two halves of the artist's brain. But just then? There was no differentiating the material. It was all still one thing, a collection of songs for the next record, waiting to be turned into recordings. Springsteen took a closer look at what he had on the cassette, asked himself why it wasn't working when they tried to rerecord it. "Light. That was my judgment on the entire success of *Nebraska*," Springsteen told me at his Colts Neck home. "What altered when we went in the studio was the light that was shining on the music and the listener. In the studio we started to fuck with the songs *because* we fucked with the light. Tremendously. The slightest alteration really ruined it. The nature of the unbelievably basic equipment that we used was just unique. When you transferred it over, brought it up to tone, and raised the faders on the professional recording gear, that's what we screwed with, we screwed with the light on the whole thing. Everything reflected differently."

Sometimes the act of songwriting isn't an act at all. It can be sitting still, waiting, listening, asking questions of a song that's already, from one perspective, done. "I went into the studio," Springsteen told me, "brought in the band to rerecord and remix those songs, and succeeded in making the whole thing worse. The characters got lost."

The characters. Not only was he unwilling to risk losing the people of *Nebraska;* he was now going to go back and find them, get to know them better. As songwriters often discover and rediscover, just because you wrote it doesn't mean you know what the hell it is right away. But once Springsteen understood that the light of the recordings, and the characters on whom that light shined, were altered in the professional recording environment, he knew better what he needed to do. He needed to find a way to preserve those very things, the light and the characters.

Only when he saw what the Colts Neck recordings *couldn't* be did he really begin to see what they were. And with that, the album that would become *Born in the U.S.A.* was officially put on the shelf, where it would languish for well over a year. "The album of *Born in the U.S.A.*," Jon Landau told me, "the dimension of it, the universal aspect of it that could take his career to a scale that was unprecedented for him, absolutely never would have come to exist without *Nebraska*. But I think he was the only one who saw that then, if even he did."

———

Another aspect of the Colts Neck recordings that seemed to recede from view when the songs were rerecorded at the Power Station was the context and backdrop, the time when he made them and the America he felt around him when he pressed record. Springsteen wasn't involved in reportage, but he was out to capture the stillness, a certain American hopelessness he believed was obscured by the saturated colors animating President Reagan's vision of the country. Somewhere in the rough, unfinished quality of the recordings he located an otherwise hidden America, one he knew needed to be exposed.

The Reagan era had ushered in a conservatism and hyperconsumerism. Deregulation allowed unchecked growth for already powerful institutions, and those who stood to benefit tended not to hesitate in taking what they could get. The divide between the very wealthy and the very poor would grow, and it would define American life in new and lasting ways.

Springsteen's worry about the increasing distance between himself and the people he was writing about brought some urgency to the task of songwriting.

Greil Marcus, writing during the *River* Tour and also thinking of Reagan's election, felt the political situation in the United States would surely reveal itself in whatever Springsteen did next, after *The River.* In a prophetic passage, Marcus insisted that "it is an almost certain bet that the songs Springsteen will now be writing will have something to do with the events of November 4. Those songs likely will not comment on those events; they will, I think, reflect those events back to us, fixing moods and telling stories that are, at present, out of reach."

When the songs from the Colts Neck sessions were eventually released as *Nebraska,* many critics and listeners would believe, as Marcus had in his vision, that the material bore some crucial relationship to its political moment, whether that was there in the literal content or not. And, when Springsteen finally spoke publicly about *Nebraska,* he wouldn't disagree. He would, however, make the point that the characters he had created, who seemed to whisper so many secrets about Reagan's America, didn't come from Reagan's America, even if their situations and struggles gave them a symbolic home there.

In 1984, speaking about *Nebraska* with *Hot Press,* Springsteen said, "I just had a certain tone in mind, which I felt was the tone of what it was like when I was a kid growing up. And at the same time it felt like the tone of what the country was like at the time." The characters, as he describes them, are from a *then* and a *now.* When the band fired up, and those characters "got lost," the songs stopped working as songs. And, with that, both Reagan's America and Springsteen's childhood disappeared from view.

"Sometimes the record or the film or the painting talks back to you," Jon Landau said to me, recalling this moment. "It's got its own voice, if you're listening. With our efforts to rerecord, something was not happening that was supposed to be happening. And in those moments you can't will it into working. Bruce was still listening to those songs, even after writing them."

"After starting *Born in the U.S.A.*," Toby Scott recalls, "we had to go back and address the other songs he wanted to do, which were more single-artist-type songs. At first Bruce would go out and sit on a stool and play acoustic guitar, singing those songs, and it just didn't sound like the demos. He got frustrated, and I remember there was a point in time when he told me, 'Don't come into the studio tomorrow.'" That was about as close as one might get to the precise moment it happened: a decision was reached. And when Toby Scott came back to work, the focus had shifted.

The failed attempts to rerecord the songs threw Springsteen into a momentary uncertainty. Then, somewhere along the line, someone said, "Why don't you just put out those demos?" Maybe that cassette in his pocket, the one with lint on it that he'd been carrying around, *was the record*. Chuck Plotkin believes it was Jon Landau's idea to release the cassette. But Landau credits Springsteen. Steven Van Zandt says it was his idea.

When I asked Springsteen about this tangle of credits, he just looked at me, smiled in a way that suggested such a tangle wasn't the first he'd seen, and said, "Ultimately, it would have been my idea. First of all, it wasn't something that someone else *could* say. Once you get to that place, that's kind of my decision. And so it was like, here it is. *Nebraska* made its own call. The music itself decided that it was going to come out as it was. Yes, there would have been a discussion about it. But obviously, like I said, I pulled it out of my pocket one day and said, 'I think this is it.'"

CHAPTER THIRTEEN

Lost in Translation

But you have to make sure the technology doesn't outpace the humanity. . . . It didn't matter if a studio was a shiny, state-of-the-art outfit or a raggedy little room whose jerry-rigged equipment was held together with tape and whatever else was on hand: magic was laid down for the rest of the world to hear.

—QUINCY JONES, foreword to *Temples of Sound*

"At what point did Bruce think, or had he thought all along, of making the demos into an album?" Jon Landau asked, thinking out loud. "Albums are more often found, by trying things. They don't just appear. I'm not sure I, or anyone, could pinpoint the day *Nebraska* was found. It was a process." Part of that process, of course, involved getting to a point at which releasing the demos seemed a credible choice rather than a misguided one. "I guess the thing that we're touching on," Landau continued, "is how much were we acknowledging that putting out *Nebraska*—the *Nebraska* album was such an unusual and unique thing to release—was actually a crazy thing to do. How much was there an original intention to do that, and how much did it just evolve?"

But just because Springsteen had pulled that cassette from

his pocket and said, "I think this is it," that didn't mean that the "process" was over. For a minute there, an idea came into Springsteen's mind: Why not make it a double album, take the material destined for *Born in the U.S.A.* and build a second disc, a band recording, around that? It would be like two worlds with a spine connecting them. Or separating them, depending on one's perspective.

"*Born in the U.S.A.*, that album," Springsteen tells me, "initially came side by side with *Nebraska*. The first songs I cut for *Born in the U.S.A.* were *Nebraska* songs. I think I was coming off of 'Stolen Car,' out of that side of *The River*, those narrative stories. I was feeling like that was pretty interesting. So I was looking to sort of go in that vein for a while and see where it was going to take me. And it took me into the *Nebraska* record. 'Stolen Car,' that probably could have been on *Nebraska*. It was close. 'Born in the U.S.A.' came from that same period but in time differentiated itself, at least as the full band version. That was just another thing altogether."

The two albums were initially so oddly intertwined that separating them was, at least early, a significant part of the creative work. Much later Springsteen would almost wish he'd left some trace of the interconnectedness of the two. One album, *Born in the U.S.A.*, would live under a hundred spotlights; the other, *Nebraska*, would watch from the shadows. "My big mistake," he insisted, "was leaving the *Nebraska* version of 'Born in the U.S.A.' off of *Nebraska*. I should have put it on there. I could have easily had it on both records. It would have made complete sense, and it would have been a fine part of the *Nebraska* record. It fit perfectly."

Of course, that was thinking done in hindsight, and likely affected by the various, almost willful misinterpretations of "Born in the U.S.A." that would, in time, celebrate the song as a patriotic anthem of some kind. Ronald Reagan's nod to "Born in the U.S.A." and the man who wrote it is only the best-known example of an interpretative effort that was, in effect, more like a hijacking. The applause was mighty and Reagan's people were comfortable looking right past the world of trouble inside "Born in the U.S.A." Yes, they made a practice of looking past wreckage. But if "Born in the U.S.A." had been on *Nebraska,* things might have been different. No flag on the cover, no snare to rouse a generation.

But the double album idea didn't last long. No doubt that was due in part to some lingering double album fatigue. *The River* was still too close. Double albums, even the greatest among them, more often began their lives as the solution to a problem rather than as an idea in and of themselves. But in solving one problem, double albums often created others. Springsteen didn't need to visit that place again.

So a choice was made. *Nebraska* would end up being the only official release in Springsteen's catalog that was made without Springsteen's knowing he was making a record. That sound, the one of an artist unaware that he's making an album, couldn't be replicated at the Power Station. The sound of not-knowingness, the sound of isolation, can't be consciously reproduced. If he had been sitting on the end of his bed in the Colts Neck rental thinking he was making a record, everything—the mood, the mistakes, the voice, the mixing decisions, the time it took— would have been different. Springsteen was beginning to understand what he had, what those songs were, why they sounded the way they did, what had gone right.

> SPRINGSTEEN: I had to lay myself way out there. I really had to do it. Mike was invisible in the room. It was like being there by myself. I had all the freedom that I needed, as if I was there on my own. That's how that record got made.
>
> WZ: Together with that firm knowledge that you were definitely not making a record.
>
> SPRINGSTEEN: Not making a record. That's very important.
>
> WZ: You'll never be able to reproduce those conditions.
>
> SPRINGSTEEN: No, you can't do that.
>
> WZ: So *The Ghost of Tom Joad* will be a comparison, but it doesn't share that fundamental aspect.
>
> SPRINGSTEEN: Even if you got the same gear, that's just not the way it would work. It happened once. By accident. The second time you do it, the scene gets crowded with intention.

What Springsteen didn't see coming, however, was the problem of translation, of getting the mixes on the cassette tape, which spoke one language, onto a piece of vinyl, which had its own mother tongue. A few machines would have to talk to one another across formats. And what seemed straightforward in that regard turned out not to be straightforward at all. It was an issue that would plague creators as mediums, formats, and technologies would come and go with increasing regularity. The digital age would begin as a kind of pileup. For weeks the whole *Nebraska* album was, yet again, an uncertainty. It started to seem as if the recordings Springsteen had made were entombed in a cassette tape . . . inaccessible to anyone else.

Chuck Plotkin would be put in charge of the rescue operation. But even weeks into that effort, he had found no solution. He went to Springsteen, nothing good to report. Plotkin remembers it as the only time he saw Springsteen appear to be crying.

Chuck Plotkin was like many on Springsteen's team: he came in for a job he hadn't trained for, that of mixer, and then stayed.

It was Jon Landau who brought Plotkin in a few years before *Nebraska,* maybe because Landau knew Springsteen even better than he realized. They needed someone to mix *Darkness on the Edge of Town,* and Plotkin wasn't a mixer. Perfect. But it wouldn't have happened in quite the same way without Harry Chapin inadvertently playing a key role.

Harry Chapin is best remembered for 1974's "Cat's in the Cradle," a melodrama in song form. It's not the kind of material or production that earned great love from music critics in the rock era. Jon Landau, then overseeing reviews at *Rolling Stone,* wrote one tough review of a Chapin project. After that, he assigned Chapin's recordings to other writers. "I did see that he was doing this great work on the issue of world hunger," Landau explains. "And he was a very charismatic guy, as I found out when he called me up and asked if he could come see me. Which he did, bringing his guitar along with him."

Despite the bad review, Chapin told Landau that he always

liked reading the critic's writing, and now that Landau was a record producer, well, maybe they could work together. Landau listened to some of Chapin's material, but he knew he had the follow-up to *Born to Run* coming. Landau suggested that Chapin talk to Chuck Plotkin. True to his word, Landau then turned his attention to the project that would become *Darkness on the Edge of Town*. They were going to fight with that one for many months, well over a year.

When they were finally ready to mix *Darkness on the Edge of Town,* by that time working at the Record Plant, no one in the room was of one mind. Landau, Springsteen, Steven Van Zandt, Jimmy Iovine: they all had different ideas. "We couldn't mix the record," Landau says. "We were stymied. We were working on 'Prove It All Night,' getting nowhere. So, I got an idea in my head: I call Chuck Plotkin in L.A. His assistant at Elektra/Asylum tells me Chuck is actually in New York. 'Oh, that's great,' I say. 'Where can I get ahold of him?' The assistant tells me that he's at the Record Plant, the studio we were sitting in, on the tenth floor, producing Harry Chapin."

Making his way to the tenth floor, Landau found Plotkin and said he needed help. It was only nine floors by elevator for Plotkin to unknowingly enter a new phase in his life and career. The biggest yet. Plotkin recalls the moment:

> Jon Landau comes to me and says, "Charlie, I could use your help with something here. We've been working on this record for quite some time." The record turned out to be *Darkness on the Edge of Town*. Jon tells me they're not finding the sound they're after. "All we got is dull or shrill,"

he says. "We can't have dull or shrill. Would you stop by and just listen?" So I stop by. Everything's done. They're just mixing. And the person mixing at that point is somebody who was a much better mixer than I would ever become: Jimmy Iovine. But when I stepped into this project, when Jon asked me to come by, Jimmy looked like he belonged in a hospital. They were working these crazy hours, beating themselves up, trying to do something that they felt they were failing at.

"I said to Jon, 'Okay, here's my story,'" Plotkin recalls. "'You know I'm not a mixer. I know I'm not a mixer. I'm not even a recording engineer. If the tape on a multitrack machine rolled off at the end, I wouldn't know how to reload it.'" No matter. Landau, Van Zandt, Iovine, and Springsteen left Plotkin at the studio with the engineer Thom Panunzio, giving Plotkin a couple of hours to come up with a mix of "Prove It All Night."

"We come back in," recalls Landau, "listen to 'Prove It All Night.' Bruce turns to me and says, 'That's the best my music has ever sounded.'" Plotkin, not one to sing his own praises, and this in an industry that's always breaking new ground in the area of self-aggrandizement, tells me that the solutions he arrived at in his mix weren't beyond the reach of the others. "Except that they were burnt," Plotkin insists. "Exhausted and frustrated."

"I wasn't a Bruce fan," says Plotkin. "I'd never seen Bruce live. I wouldn't have recognized him on the street. This was about my relationship with Jon. Then the music took over." The next song was "Adam Raised a Cain." This time, Springsteen, sitting beside Plotkin at the console, set it up. "Bruce starts by saying, 'This one's very different,'" remembers Plotkin. "'Adam Raised a Cain' was this dark, strange thing," he recalls.

Bruce says, "Let me tell you a little something about this one." He wasn't going to sit through the entire process of mixing, but he wanted to set the scene. Part of what he must have realized was that I could have gotten the wrong idea for how to proceed with "Adam Raised a Cain" based on everyone's enthusiasm for how "Prove It All Night" sounded. He knew this thing couldn't sound anything like that, and probably realized he needed to give me some assistance. "It's a movie," he tells me. "We're in a park. There's a couple, and they're deeply in love, very engaged with each other. It's dark. Or getting dark. And then, at some point, there's a shock cut to a mutilated dead body that's lying like twenty feet from where the couple is." He says, "I want you to think of this song as the mutilated dead body. I want the listener to experience that mutilated dead body every time they hear this."

Chuck Plotkin quit his job at Elektra/Asylum soon after. By the time of *Born in the U.S.A.*, he was listed among the album's producers. For *Nebraska*? His role was second only to Springsteen's. Again, it was Plotkin who would have to find a way to get the music recorded on the TEAC 144 onto vinyl. The CD era was beginning but only just. For the most part, the audience was going to listen to *Nebraska* as an LP—if Plotkin could find a way to get it there. As a concept, moving recorded music from one place to the other seemed entirely plausible, like something that happened all the time.

———

Part of what makes recording studios somewhat odd, a little museum-like in spirit, is that the gear of the past is not always rendered obsolete, even as the very latest technologies are welcomed in. A Telefunken U47 microphone from the 1940s is a favorite among artists across genres. Still. A Fairchild 670 compressor from the 1950s—they can cost some thirty thousand dollars on the vintage market—is regularly used in the digital environments of today's best commercial studios. "There is a mystical air about a Fairchild 670," Pete Townshend has said. "Sorry, but that's a fact." Old technologies, mythic technologies, and the very latest gear mix together in a way that is singular to recording culture. With the shift from analog to digital recording, the mixing of old and new would be ever more conspicuous and common.

Imagine an office in which individual workstations have equipment from different eras: a typewriter in one, a Macintosh from 1985 in the next, and, in the following cubicle, a MacBook Pro from 2022. It wouldn't happen. When the new stuff comes in, the old goes out. Computers, printers, copiers. In a recording studio, because different eras of technology do come together, a common language must be found.

What made the TEAC 144 alien in the commercial recording environment, however, wasn't its age. It was its status as a consumer model. In the early 1980s, consumer and professional recording equipment had little in common and weren't created to interact. There was a caste system. Consumer and commercial gear didn't frequent the same joints. Chuck Plotkin:

> One of the things about *Nebraska* is it's cut on a crap piece of equipment. It wasn't a proper recording setup. It was also recorded by somebody who'd never recorded anything before. But they were making demos, so that wasn't an issue. Then at some point it becomes clear that our efforts to re-record the songs are not serving the material, that there's something magical about this demo Bruce has made. And we have to confront the fact that instead of carrying on trying some other approach to bring back the magic—maybe we have the magic. So what are we trying to do? I just had to make it releasable. But then we're in this situation where we bring a TEAC 144 into a professional studio.

Toby Scott recalls the confusion of tongues:

> Bruce brought that four-track machine in, and we had the guy from the Power Station modify it so we had four individual outputs. They transferred a bunch of these songs from the cassette onto two-inch tape, thinking, "Maybe he can play along with himself." Nothing worked. The further we got into it, the more we discovered that there were too many variables and variations.

The TEAC 144 presented Springsteen and his team with something as strange as they'd ever worked with. "We had a lot of unique audio issues," Landau recalls. "Bruce is walking around with a cassette, his follow-up to *The River* on it. He gave me the cassette when he wanted me to hear the songs. I mean, I didn't know what we were heading into. I played it and gave it back to him, and the thing just kept coming back. Then, when we agreed to work from the demos, they refused our efforts to transfer the audio in some fashion that made sense to us." The biggest name in American rock and roll, surrounded by a team as fine as any at work in popular music, and they couldn't get a thing past this cassette tape.

Springsteen had already decided on releasing the music from the cassette, but even he imagined a process of cleaning up the audio. Now it seemed even that wouldn't be possible. Toby Scott remembers the return of the cassette.

> That's when Bruce is standing in the studio and pulls the cassette out of his pocket, holds it up, and says, "What's the chance of mastering directly from this?" At which point Chuck and Jon both groan. Because here it was, mastering from a cassette you'd buy at Walgreens. Bruce said, "What else are we gonna do?"

"Even this much conventionalizing, trying to transfer the four-track recordings to something better, wasn't working," Plotkin explains. "We'd done *again* what we did by going into the studio and trying to rerecord everything with the band. We've made everything clean, clear, lovely sounding. And it suffered. First we find we can't rerecord it; then we find we can't even remix it."

This didn't happen in an afternoon. "We stopped remixing," Plotkin recalls. "And this was already like weeks into the process. At that point we have to acknowledge that the mixes are on that cassette of Bruce's. All the echo he put on will have to stay. I'm going to have to go in and master from that. Okay, so I knew I needed to go to Bob Ludwig, who's one of the very best mastering engineers if not the best."

The process of record making goes in those stages: recording, mixing, mastering. With this cassette, they found they couldn't intervene on the first two stages. There was one left, mastering. The mastering process involved equalization and compression, which could increase the clarity and power of a mix. Maybe there, Plotkin thought, the audio quality of these performances could be enhanced. Among the mastering engineers who handled the biggest commercial projects in the rock era, a few names would show up more than others. Greg Calbi, Stephen Marcussen, Bob Ludwig. It made sense that Plotkin went to Bob Ludwig.

> I went to Bob, and he's not all that enthusiastic. It's going to have his name on it after it's all done. And people will be wondering what happened. It's still not going to sound like other major releases. Why would Bob expect Bruce's next record to come in on a cassette? But he did it for us. And what happened is it came back on disc—in those days you would do the mastering onto a disc—and it distorted. If you listened carefully to the master you could hear a kind of distortion. Somehow the mastering emphasized this distortion.

Word got back to Springsteen as various attempts were made to master the recordings. Once he'd decided that the mixed demos should be released, he'd gotten more and more set on the idea. Plotkin let Springsteen and Landau know that he'd keep trying. "I think he had to go to three, four, maybe five mastering facilities," Toby Scott recalls. "I know he went to Ludwig, and out to L.A., to Steve Marcussen, and then he may have taken it to Bernie Grundman, and maybe to Sterling." False hopes were sprinkled throughout the process.

"For my second stop I went to a guy I trusted, Steve Marcussen, good ears," Plotkin explains. "He cuts a disc, and this time it plays back fine. It sounds great. We're listening back on his seventeen-thousand-dollar turntable. So we're excited. I call Bruce, let him know I'll be back in New York in two days, that I've got some great news." But Plotkin, thrilled to be able to play Springsteen a successful master, didn't play it back on a seventeen-thousand-dollar turntable. "I put the thing on for Bruce," Plotkin recalls, "and it's crap sound in all the same spots as Bob Ludwig's master. Bruce is like . . . well, I'd known him for a while, and we were becoming friends. But I could tell he was fighting back the tears."

Landau, hearing about the latest problems with the cassette, couldn't help but think about the fact that two-thirds of *Born in the U.S.A.* was sitting on the shelf as this quest unfolded. But he responded to Springsteen's unwavering commitment to the Colts Neck recordings, as did Plotkin. "Chuck was meticulous and deeply attentive," Landau says. "The word 'stubborn' doesn't even begin to describe Chuck. He's outrageous. We have to take that into account when we're working with him.

But *Nebraska* wouldn't have gotten made if Chuck hadn't kept at it."

"Bruce didn't say this after I played the second bad master," Plotkin says, "but he was so clearly thinking, 'What the hell, I make this recording with my guitar, my own home equipment, and after weeks of trying to better it in a studio, we all have to conclude that not only are my home recordings more compelling than anything we're managing to do in the fancy studio but now that we know we have to use them . . . we *can't*? Now what? Do we throw them out?'" Finally, it was old gear that saved them.

Atlantic Records had its own studio. But with the rise of independent operations like the Hit Factory and the Power Station, artists tended to use the label-owned studios less. Because of that, Atlantic's facility wasn't the busiest place in town or the most cutting edge. Where other operations upgraded to automated lathes for mastering, Atlantic had not. Dennis King, mastering engineer at the studio, still had to adjust the depth and distance between grooves on a disc by hand, the old way. But when he did, finally something worked. The old gear seemed to be able to talk to the cheap gear.

The only hitch was that this worked only when the disc was cut at a low audio level, which bothered Plotkin far more than it bothered Springsteen. Years before, while mastering *Darkness on the Edge of Town,* Springsteen had to choose between keeping the long fade he wanted on "Racing in the Street" or having equal audio levels on both sides of the album. He chose the long fade, leaving one side of *Darkness* slightly quieter than the other. Springsteen's response: "They have volume knobs, right?"

"We had no choice," Plotkin recalled. "That's all we could do. We had to cut this at an incredibly low level so that the needle wasn't digging too deeply into the material, the vinyl. Way lower." Landau stood somewhere between Plotkin and Springsteen: "Well, I feel sure that Bruce himself didn't care about the record being quiet. Chuck cared because as a professional he wanted the record to have strength. He wanted this so that when a person at home is playing records and *Nebraska* comes on, that person doesn't feel like they have to raise the volume to make it on par with the record they were just listening to."

Thinking of the cassette tape that took over his life for a time, Plotkin recalls the anomalous nature of the thing: "The strange choice of instruments. The strange sound of his voice into this microphone. The strange sound of cassette tape mixed to a cassette tape. Two generations of cassette tapes. Whenever I talked to Jon, he assured me, 'This is going to get put out without a single, and it's going to be without a tour. We're in there making the next rock record right now, and it's going to be an important release. But in the meantime, Bruce has made this.' Keeping that in mind was obviously important. We had to trust Bruce and see that bigger picture." Years later, it would seem *Nebraska* was the pulling back of the bow, and *Born in the U.S.A.* was the arrow's release. But that one-two effect was, just then, still only a feeling, an article of faith.

For Plotkin, it was a lesson in who this artist was. This experience was different from any he'd seen in his long career. "Bruce was not simply brave enough to do this sort of thing, but was compelled to do this sort of thing," Plotkin said.

What an artist has to do to keep himself alive as an artist is to not get stuck. Bruce was always more concerned about whether or not he could maintain an authentic relationship to his own experience and to his audience than whether this sold or reached this number on the charts. At some point he had more money than he could possibly do anything with anyway, unless he was going to give it all away, but he grew up too poor for that. From what I remember of being close enough to the heart of what was going on at that time, in the artistic and personal realm, was that he— and it's always hard all these decades later to remember for sure if this is how he voiced it or if this is how I sensed it— but he actually found himself saying that this was the first completely honest piece of work that he'd ever done. And at that point he was looking back on some very good stuff. But he had this sense that he had never caught the thing by its tail. Even I would have people come up to me at shows after the release of *Nebraska*. Complete fans. I don't even know how they recognized me. But they'd come up and say, "Oh, God, this is the music."

The various producers involved with the previous few albums, Landau, Plotkin, Springsteen, and Steven Van Zandt, were all connected with *Nebraska* in some way. But none of them would be credited as producers. "Retrospectively," Landau says, "I would say that a record which had such a special way of coming into being, well, that even putting 'Produced by Bruce Springsteen' didn't feel right to Bruce. There's certainly nobody else you could give that title to. But even Bruce didn't take it for himself. So there's no producer."

"One of the things," Plotkin insists, "is that it's an acknowledgment that there's something precious about Bruce being able to work in an environment where, hey, there's no real equipment. He's writing about the middle of the night, and he's singing about it *in* the middle of the night. All by himself. He's not evaluating his performances, he's just blowing it out. That's *Nebraska*. It's like the battle to expose. That business of the authenticity of the experiences he was reporting on is critical. There's some complex thing at work in the relationship between an artist and himself, an artist and his audience that just . . . it's wild, it's challenging. I'd never see it again like I saw it with *Nebraska*."

With a completed master, it was now time to take it to the record label, to tell the executives, "Here's the next Bruce Springsteen release." Rough home demos. Mastered at a low level. No singles. First track is about a serial killer. No tour or press. If you could make a list of the things a record company does *not* want to hear . . .

CHAPTER FOURTEEN

Taking It to the Label

America has always been the home of hucksterism and extreme salesmanship.

—Russell Banks, *Dreaming Up America*

oto, Men at Work, Earth, Wind & Fire, Barbra Streisand, Judas Priest, Cher, Paul McCartney, Journey. There were things going on at Columbia Records. None of it sounded like *Nebraska*. When a major act brought in a new recording, it was often a moment of celebration. Sometimes a track stepped right up and announced itself as a hit. Just then it was Toto's "Rosanna." McCartney's duet with Stevie Wonder, "Ebony and Ivory." Men at Work's "Who Can It Be Now?" Tommy Tutone's "867-5309/Jenny." Columbia Records was Columbia Records, so it had some familiarity with hits. The executives at the label banked on them.

There were also "prestige" artists, most notably Bob Dylan. The situation there was different. Singles or not, big album sales or not: he was a major asset to the label. And then there were prestige artists who were also capable of generating hits, like McCartney. In some way, Bruce Springsteen was already in that category. He'd only had one top ten single, but there was a feeling that more were on the way. And he was bankable even without hits. His touring history reflected it. FM radio loved him. So there was an air of anticipation around what this artist would be doing next.

By 1982, Bruce Springsteen was also well past the point at which Columbia Records was going to reject his proposed latest release. From Columbia's perspective, there was no point in risking the relationship. So, when his newest recording was delivered, it wasn't a matter of getting approval. It was a matter of presentation: *here's the new one.* But that doesn't mean label executives couldn't be confused. Or frustrated. Or a little pissed off. There would be some theater involved, no doubt. The biting of tongues. Only a few seconds into hearing *Nebraska* and any executive would know this wasn't going to be a thing of radio hits, let alone radio *play.*

Accounts differ regarding how the man running CBS Records, Walter Yetnikoff, received *Nebraska.* The journalist Fred Goodman uses the word "disappointed": "The rough-hewn album did not cheer CBS Records head Walter Yetnikoff, who, while grateful to have any new Bruce Springsteen record, would have preferred one the company could actually market. As he recounted later, he viewed it as an album 'you made in your garage, thank you. We'll do the best we can.'" It is, however, hard to find another source supporting this view of Yetnikoff's response to *Nebraska.*

The Columbia executives certainly cared about the bottom

line, but they also knew plenty about the shape of long careers as opposed to those built on a quick rise and fall. There were albums that did something over the long term that couldn't be measured with an accountant's year-end tools. And to be fair to the executives at Columbia: *Nebraska* wasn't something they could have planned for. Springsteen was giving them an album that would need to be explained to its audience, but the artist wasn't even going to let them do *that*. At Springsteen's insistence, this wasn't going to be packaged with an apology or half-hearted mumbling or even interviews to set it up. It was his new record. Period. Let the listeners figure it out. This was not the usual situation at Columbia, and that, at least, was surely clear to Yetnikoff. But the executive had other matters distracting him.

Speaking of his time at the label, Walter Yetnikoff later shared this with *The New York Times:* "'I'd come out of a coma around 7 or 8 a.m.,' he said, describing his daily routine as president of CBS Records from 1975 to 1990. 'By 9 I might have drunk a half a bottle of vodka. Then I would call someone at CBS, maybe the head of the network or accounting, and yell at them. I'd finally drag myself out of bed and get into the office around noon. The steward would immediately bring me a screwdriver.'" This suggests that *Nebraska* might not have been the most pressing matter in Yetnikoff's life at the time. The second-in-command at CBS, Al Teller, however, had fewer obstacles on the way to work *and* a history with Springsteen.

Al Teller was at Columbia when Springsteen's debut was released, before leaving to run United Artists. He'd watched from afar but with an investment in Springsteen's unfolding career. And it happened along the lines of what he'd hoped for. *Born to Run, Darkness on the Edge of Town, The River.* It was a build, solid and steady. Teller was back at Columbia just before *Nebraska* was delivered. The next Springsteen release would ultimately come to him. Walter Yetnikoff would hear it first, but Teller would be the follow-through. Landau recalls:

> I invited Walter over to my office. I start playing *Nebraska.* Just me and him sitting in my office. Which was a nothing office. And he gets it. He really gets it. In his own way. He doesn't get it in a high literary way, he doesn't get it in a nuanced way, but he gets the mood, gets the feeling. He looks at me, no hesitation, "This is great." There was no resistance to it. Then Al [Teller] comes in. I hadn't worked with Al. But I leave Al to listen to it. This guy is going to do operations for me. He says, "Jon, I'm gonna tell you two things. One, I don't understand this record. I don't even fully understand why an artist would make this record." Then he says, "Number two, I promise you we're going to do a beautiful job on it. We're going to handle this record exactly the way you want. We're not going to try to make something of it that it's not."

Al Teller had a rare gift: he said what he thought, spoke his truth. He didn't tell Landau he could smell a hit. The unexpectedness of it wasn't lost on him. Anyone who pretended that *Nebraska* made sense in the marketplace was lying. Teller's style was to go light on the style. As a result, perhaps not every artist manager had Al Teller at the top of the holiday gift list. Backslapping and bullshit were the standard. But Landau liked him. "He was just straight ahead," Landau explained. "I was a hot-head back then, or so I've been told. That was the era, the '70s, '80s. Who could yell the loudest was a big factor. But what am I going to do, explain *Nebraska* to him? It wouldn't make any difference. He was already saying, 'I'll do my job well. I'm giving you my word.' He told you what he thought and that was fine with me as long as he brought the hammer down when he was supposed to, and he did."

"I took a moment and listened to it," Al Teller recalls, "and a few things were clear to me instantly. Number one, that ever-expanding commercial balloon that was the trilogy of *Born to Run, Darkness,* and *The River* was not going to keep expanding with this one. This was a complete and total left turn." But he was still listening when those first thoughts struck him.

By the time Teller finished listening to the album, the Columbia executive had an understanding of *Nebraska* that would serve label and manager. Really, it was just a matter of getting to work. Landau's strategy, which might not have been a strategy at all, was working. Let people have their experiences. He'd watched a cassette have its way with everyone around him—why stop now? Why do a big setup? The conversation was succinct, two men in alignment. Teller had his way of understanding *Nebraska,* and it would become more nuanced, so Landau didn't need to impose one on him. Teller saw it like this:

To me it was a work of poetry as opposed to a big-time recording. I knew we wouldn't be able to treat it as other than what it was. That's what I told Jon. There's this person in me saying, "We're not going to sell three, four, five million copies of this. We might sell a half a million, maybe less, maybe more. So be it. This is an artist whose career is going to be very long-lived. This is what he chose to do at this moment in time, and we're going to respect that and handle the marketing of it appropriately, not try and do things that are simply not going to work." But it didn't take long for me to see this as a smart, smart move. Between *Born to Run, Darkness,* and *The River,* these were big productions, lots of music, big sounds, and big successes. If people were expecting that balloon to continue to expand, it was going to just blow up. You just can't keep doing that. I thought Bruce was really smart. Of course, I don't know if he did this intentionally. I don't think he approached things that way.

Al Teller's way of thinking about *Nebraska*'s place in the sequence of Springsteen's releases is enough to make one consider whether it was an orchestrated career strategy. To go from "Hungry Heart" to "Dancing in the Dark" might have done more damage than good. *Nebraska* got the critics on board, made a bold statement about art before *Born in the U.S.A.* stormed the marketplace. There's something satisfying in the composition of such a picture, something about an artist showing the scope of his territories in just two records. Beggar to king. In that vision, *Nebraska* is the stripping back of all ornament. Throw out the rich hues, the gold leaf, and the aquamarine, just pen and ink, etchings maybe.

But it couldn't be. Too much is known to support such a story of strategy. They *tried* to make a different *Nebraska*. They just couldn't. But Teller dealt with what he had and kept its follow-up in the back of his mind. "I fully expected," he recalls, "even when we were doing the *Nebraska* album, that the next one was not going to be *Nebraska Two*."

"Jon's concern," Teller says, "was that we, as a record company, might try to do things with it that they would not have felt comfortable with." Landau hoped his Columbia team wouldn't mislead the consumer: ring the bells too loud, and they'll expect a pageant. To Columbia's credit, they didn't. The record would often have a sticker declaring that it was "the solo album." Most of the print ads looked like the album cover. Only an ad in *Melody Maker* suggests what too much might look like. "Basic / Brilliant / Solo Springsteen," it said, and then, below an image from the album's back cover, it goes further: "Nobody but Springsteen can tell stories like these / On 'Nebraska' ain't nobody but Springsteen telling 'em." Once you start the build, there's really nowhere to take it. But for the most part, CBS kept it in check. And Teller was rewarded.

CHAPTER FIFTEEN

Nowhere in Sight

I was interested in making myself as invisible as possible. I just wanted to be another ghost.

—BRUCE SPRINGSTEEN, speaking with the author in 2021

Nineteen eighty-two is as good a year as any to mark the threshold of a future we're still negotiating. It's been called the information age, the digital age, the new media age. It was the beginning of the "digital turn" that would, in fits and starts, transform music culture, whether for artists, listeners, lawyers, or those executives who for decades were, in McGuinn and Hillman's words, "waiting there to sell plasticware."

With the CD entering the marketplace, digital synthesizers and drum machines becoming more common, digital recording and sampling developing, the year of *Nebraska*'s release marked the start of the gateway era. Email, digitization, the internet: it was all in the works well before 1982, but now the digital future was getting closer to everyday life, leaving the labs for the neighborhoods. *Time*'s Man of the Year in 1982? The personal computer, the magazine's first nonhuman in that role.

It was also a moment in which the visual culture of popular music would transform almost overnight. The coinage that MTV foisted upon its early audience—"You'll never look at music the same way again"—would be hard to challenge. Jeff Ayeroff, working in the Warner Bros. art department soon after MTV's start, says, "With MTV, the art department could break an act. And this was something new." Those who resisted or dismissed the growing importance of video as a marketing tool did so only to their own detriment in the marketplace. The vast majority put in their shoulder pads and walked toward the cameras.

That more conspicuously visual music culture would drive sales in the CD era. But music video was only the most obvious trace of the coming era's scopophilia. In the next decade, with advances in digital recording, the computer screen became the locus of recording. Music would be seen. Recording engineers would assess visually the sounds they were capturing. For many of the next generation of engineers, when they would see a musical mistake—even if they hadn't first heard it—they would feel compelled to fix it. And by that time they could. That may be the biggest of the changes that lay ahead: when the eyes would go to work on the project of making . . . perfect music. "Seeing music probably wasn't a good thing," Bob Clearmountain said to me. "It was an advantage if you wanted everything to sound perfect. But a lot of people went too far with it. There's something about humans playing music. And when we could see and fix mistakes, we stopped hearing the humans. *Nebraska*? Just sounding as it did was one of its most important features."

Against the digital backdrop, *Nebraska* was going to be a lasting symbol, representing an alternative tradition. Its mistakes,
its accidental character, its imperfections: all would be a crucial
part of the album's life force and legacy. So when Springsteen
worked to create the visual elements to accompany his new
release, there too would he depart from the moment. The
flamboyance, unrestrained color, and restless pace of the MTV
1980s were nowhere in evidence.

From what Springsteen says, there wasn't a lot of deliberation when it came to the album art for *Nebraska*. "I knew I
shouldn't be on the cover," he said. "I never gave it a second
thought." Columbia's designer, Andrea Klein, hired the photographer David Michael Kennedy after showing Springsteen
some of Kennedy's work. They would do a day of shooting,
but they ended up using an image the photographer had taken
in 1975. But for Springsteen it was as much about the image as
it was the graphics that accompanied it:

> I liked the photograph she found and what was done with
> it, just the stark, red-and-black, black-and-white layout,
> and the big letters. It was all just very bloody in its own
> way. I remember a lot of work, a lot of fussing over many
> of the album covers, but I don't remember *Nebraska* being
> one of them.

On the inner sleeve Springsteen makes his only appearance,
almost as though he'd mistakenly come upon David Michael
Kennedy while passing through a room. Out of focus, in an
image of Kennedy's dominated by the presence of a doorframe

belonging to a house seemingly from the mid- to late nineteenth century, he's in motion. The interior of the home calls to mind the Hopperesque Victorian home featured in Terrence Malick's *Days of Heaven,* a mansion on a hill. But what Springsteen wanted to convey most directly on the inner sleeve image was some sense of his being there *and not being there:*

I mean, the picture we used inside, it was kind of my ghost. It wasn't quite me. It was the pre- . . . I don't know what you want to call it . . . that earlier part of yourself that stays with you. For some reason, he pulls that out of you, this photographer David Kennedy. We spent a day in a house upstate in New York somewhere, and that was it, you know? But he caught that one little ghostly picture, which worked well on the inside. I was all focused on the characters on the record, it was all about them, the ones in the songs. It wasn't about me so much. I was totally concentrated on who the people were, that world they lived in. That world was what I wanted on the cover. The world I was describing, that's what the cover needed to be.

Andrea Klein's graphic design would give all of *Nebraska's* promotional materials a strong visual identity. The video director Arnold Levine would then carry the black-and-white aesthetic over to his treatment of "Atlantic City," Springsteen's first music video.

Levine had worked on a few Springsteen-related projects, most notably a live shoot in 1978, done during the *Darkness on the Edge of Town* tour at the Veterans Memorial Coliseum in Phoenix. Earlier than that, however, at the time of Springsteen's debut, Levine also shot what might rank as Springsteen's most awkward video project, featuring Clive Davis.

"When Bruce came out with that first album," Levine recalls, "his lyrics were very strange. At the time, I was doing a lot of work with Clive, and Clive called me about this. He said, 'You need to film me giving my opinion of Bruce's record and of his lyrics because I want people to understand this is a very different artist. I want to read some of his lyrics.' He wanted to introduce Bruce to the people at radio and in the field who would be meeting Springsteen for the first time." Levine set up for a shoot in Clive Davis's office, filming the label head as he, yes, introduced Springsteen and read some of his lyrics.

"They used to sign bands what seemed like every week. Most of them would have one record, and you'd never hear from them again. Clive knew Bruce was an artist," says Levine. "So he wanted to find a way to introduce him. But to hear Clive read those lyrics . . . well, something wasn't working. It certainly introduced me to Bruce Springsteen's music, though."

By the time of *Nebraska,* things had changed. At that point Springsteen typically delivered his own products to the label, canceling out the possibility of poetry readings held by former lawyers with good intentions. The video for "Atlantic City," however, was an exception. "Particularly in those days," Springsteen says, "I was such a control nut that it was very unusual for me to hand something over for someone else to do. But he got what the feel of the record was and he went with it. Did a good job." The only directive Levine got from Springsteen was consistent with what he'd wanted for the cover: keep him out of it and make it black and white.

"It was my first video," Springsteen says. "Arnold did it

completely on his own, you know? I don't even remember us asking for it, at least initially. I seem to remember thinking it might get played as a video, but only because almost anything was getting on MTV in those days. At the outset, most any artist who had a video could get on."

It was the label that first approached Levine, knowing he had a relationship with Springsteen:

> They came to me with the idea of doing "Atlantic City."
> Bruce probably selected that, and the company supported
> it. After listening several times to the song, the idea was ob-
> viously the contrast between the *promise* of Atlantic City in
> gambling and the *reality* of Atlantic City. They built up the
> boardwalk, built up a lot of casinos. But behind the
> facade—and not too far behind it at all—it was as it always
> was. It was poor. It was run-down. It was a problem. They
> never came to fix that when they brought in the promise of
> gambling. So that was basically the idea. To go and show
> that dichotomy between boardwalks, casinos, and then
> what you found a block past that.

The paradox of a casino world, with all that separates the promise from the actual payoff: it was natural territory for a Springsteen video. Springsteen had long admired Robert Frank's book of photographs *The Americans,* which played with the American veneer and the lives that lay behind it in much the way Levine would with "Atlantic City." Springsteen had been twenty-four when he first encountered Frank's book.

"I think a friend had given me a copy—and the tone of the pictures," Springsteen recalled in *DoubleTake,* "how he gave us a look at different kinds of people, got to me in some way. I've always wished I could write songs the way he takes pictures. I think I've got half a dozen copies of that book stashed around the house, and I pull one out once in a while to get a fresh look at the photographs."

Levine and a skeleton crew went to Atlantic City for a day. They had no shooting script. The look they went for recalls handheld, cinema verité camera work. But without the star there to step into the frame, it also seems like B-roll, all environment. "No script," Levine told me. "I knew what the overall idea was, so that was the important thing. I was going in only with an idea in my head and looking for the pictures to resolve that. It was Bruce, so I knew he wanted something that was more storytelling and artful.

"What was in the back of my mind was documentary style," Levine remembers. "Color was not going to do what I wanted to do. Black and white was grittier, *more* storytelling. I just felt it was a simpler approach. I thought of Walker Evans, Farm Security Administration photography. We went from early in the morning until late at night, took the last shot, the one of the buses in that parking lot, and left. We didn't know what we'd get when the day started. But we did by day's end." It was a lack of planning that brought the video into sync with the whole of the *Nebraska* project. And when MTV put the video into rotation, Springsteen was right where he wanted to be, nowhere in sight.

A few years after its release, Springsteen would admit that *Nebraska* is about isolation. In 1982 a new isolation was coming that made *Nebraska* oddly prophetic. Yes, *Nebraska* stood apart from the gloss, color, and clean lines of 1982's releases, whether *Jane Fonda's Workout Record* or albums from A Flock of Seagulls, Stray Cats, or Lionel Richie. But, viewed in hindsight, the weather captured on *Nebraska's* cover was closer to the truth of the forecast.

The Sony Walkman had already arrived in 1979, same year as the TEAC 144, and it was another way to bring your music with you. In one writer's words, the Walkman "would revolutionize the way we listened to music in a way that no other device really had ever done before." It played a major role in making the cassette the leading format, until the CD would take over the marketplace.

More important, the Walkman got us alone with our music. Just as the personal computer would get us alone with everything else. Soon enough, social media would arrive to tell us we weren't alone. The age of information would at times offer remarkable theaters of human connection that would throw many off the scent, but the fact was that the technologies of isolation were intensifying. *Nebraska,* even if inadvertently, saw one kind of isolation coming as it looked back on another.

CHAPTER SIXTEEN

Handing It Over to the Audience

Well, the president was mentioning my name in his speech
the other day, and I kinda got to wondering what his favorite album must've been, you know? I don't think it was the
Nebraska album. I don't think he's been listening to this one.

—BRUCE SPRINGSTEEN, introducing "Johnny 99,"
Pittsburgh, September 21, 1984

Nebraska was unlike Springsteen's other releases in more ways than one. Yes, it was the only record he made not thinking he was making a record. But it was also the only record he would release and then do nothing to promote. With previous albums, Springsteen went on tour, and from the stage he could see and feel how his audience responded. That mattered to him far more than the charts, more than reviews. It was immediate, visceral feedback from the fans who were committed enough to buy not just the album but the concert ticket. From up there, Springsteen could even see what musical elements within a particular song got the strongest emotional response. It was a tremendous amount of information for a songwriter and record maker, all from the most reliable source.

As Al Teller, Jon Landau, Springsteen, and, really, everyone involved in Springsteen's career knew, *Nebraska* was going to ask a lot of the listeners. If they loved Springsteen for the sliver of hope and possibility of redemption his songs offered, they were out of luck with *Nebraska*. If they loved the sound of the E Street Band and the way Springsteen led the group, that, too, was gone. If they loved the way he produced and arranged the songs into recordings rich in dynamics, nope, it wasn't there in the same way. And there would be no live shows allowing Springsteen to find out how it was going for them, to get information directly from his fans.

Since Springsteen wasn't doing interviews, the critics receiving prerelease copies of *Nebraska* were coming at it cold. The artist didn't seed the territory, giving background, citing influences, elaborating on his ambitions and intentions, none of it. Jon Landau described to me the unusual nature of that decision:

> It's the only album, in all these years of working with him, when he didn't do one interview. And though people always say, "In a rare interview with Bruce Springsteen . . . ," interviews with Bruce are not that rare. But there's something about him that makes everybody feel like it's rare. For his other records, though, he did plenty of talking. He was always a willing part of the process. He talked to whoever the top journalist was in Denver. *Nebraska*? Nothing.

There would be magazine ads, yes, and radio would be serviced, but no one from CBS was trying to make this record perform in a way that was in opposition to the album's character. It was coming out the same year as Michael Jackson's *Thriller*, and there was no reason to compete with projects tailored to stun the marketplace. Acknowledging the unusual nature of all this, Springsteen talked to me about his assurance that in the case of *Nebraska* there could be no other way:

> It was that kind of record. I knew enough not to fuck with it, not to try and help people with it. It was yours. Once you bought it, it was yours. You were going to have your own journey through it, and I didn't want to screw with what your trip was going to be. Whether I was going to do interviews or tour behind it wasn't something I remember having a lot of discussions about. I just didn't want to explain it. I thought I could only hurt the project at that moment by trying to explain it . . . if I *could* explain it. Like I said, it was sort of an accident. I didn't want to talk about it. It would have been bad voodoo at that moment, would have been bad magic for the record. I believed that if I'm interested in it, they'll be interested in it. It's the Martin Scorsese quote, something like, "Your job as an artist is to make the audience care about your obsessions." His great films have come when he's done that. My good songs are when I've done that. So I was confident that I could do this. I could make my audience care about these people and stories and this kind of record.

But given all that Springsteen *wasn't* doing to set up the album, one of the few measures for how it was doing after its release would be the charts. Just as the fans and critics didn't have a lot to go on, neither did Springsteen. The lines of communication, outside what Springsteen was saying through the songs themselves, were closed. If the charts weren't Springsteen's go-to assessment tool under normal conditions, it had to be acknowledged that these weren't normal conditions. The charts were one place he could look to see if this quiet release was surviving amid the noise, high gloss, and glamour of the "hit parade." Could something without all of the rollout and fanfare and ornament find a place, no matter its hushed tones? Jon Landau recalls the moment:

> He calls me after it's been out for a bit and asks, "How's the album doing?" I said, "It's doing great, it's fantastic." "No," he said, "what's it doing on the charts?" And that's a question, well . . . that's the only time he ever asked me that. I tell him when there's something to tell him, but he's satisfied with "Hey, it's doing great." He doesn't need the details. So I told him it was number three, which it was. It was in the top ten. He said, "Fantastic. That's great. Talk to you later." So that's *Nebraska*. He wouldn't promote it. But he cared utterly about how it went down. And it was a success.

When I shared Landau's recollection with Springsteen, he said, "That's interesting. I guess I never thought a lot about where a record was on the charts. But I do know that I just wanted . . . I was very invested in the record's reception. Not to know I was selling a lot of records, not to know if it was or wasn't a big record—I knew it wasn't—but just to understand something about the way that people were experiencing it. I was very interested in that." He was watching from afar, something he'd never done with a record. Peering through the branches, unseen.

When *Nebraska* was released on September 30, 1982, John Cougar's "Jack and Diane" was at number one on the pop charts. *American Fool* was a big commercial success that year, and Cougar, soon to be John Cougar Mellencamp, then John Mellencamp, would remain a presence on the charts with his next few releases. He was regularly compared to Springsteen, though that didn't tend to cut both ways.

"Jack and Diane," as a tale of a young American couple, was the sugarcoated cousin to Springsteen's "Nebraska." One was a fun night at the high school dance, with a trace of melancholy, the other a trip to the morgue. Yet, while standing so far apart from each other, when compared with what else was in the top ten around that time, Mellencamp's hit was akin to gritty social realism. Both Springsteen and Mellencamp were writing about America. Mellencamp's view of America, however, tilted more toward nostalgia than it did violence and isolation. *Rolling Stone* gave Springsteen's album four and a half stars, Mellencamp's two.

The critical reception of *Nebraska* was largely built on superlatives. It landed at number three on the *Village Voice* Pazz & Jop Critics Poll that year. No small deal back then. It was in there with Elvis Costello and Richard and Linda Thompson, just ahead of King Sunny Adé, Prince, and Lou Reed. Springsteen's relationship with the community of rock critics was deep and complicated. For a decade they'd been sniffing around the place, equal parts awe, celebration, suspicion, and marvel.

There had been no community of rock critics in the early rock and roll years, in the time of Elvis Presley on Sun Records and Little Richard on Specialty. But with the founding of *Rolling Stone, Crawdaddy,* and *Creem,* and even some of the teen magazines where writers could sometimes insert a story about the New York Dolls alongside those focused on David Cassidy, a generation of critics stepped forward both as tastemakers and as personalities. Lester Bangs remains the most mythologized, but he wasn't working alone. In some cases, the writers who came up in those years became managers and biographers. Meaning, Jon Landau and Dave Marsh. Springsteen would be a favorite to many, but not all.

Bruce Pollock, writing for *The New York Times* in 1973, described Springsteen's debut as a release that "met with the most extravagant and outrageous praise I've ever encountered in the Rock Press." There would be critics who couldn't help but take pride in going in the other direction. Nick Kent, in his 1974 review of Springsteen's sophomore recording, declared that Springsteen "sings like he wants you to believe a lot of things which don't quite ring true, and maybe that's why I FIND HIM SO OFFENSIVE." He was giving voice to the inevitable backlash that would often follow any praise too grand. And Springsteen knew grand praise as well as any musician of his century.

But *Nebraska* made it almost impossible for critics to miss Springsteen's willingness to take a chance in the name of his art. If Springsteen was driven simply by fame and mainstream success, there would have been no good reason to make or release a *Nebraska*. The album made it impossible to use the word "sellout." As Jon Young wrote in *Trouser Press*, "When an artist makes his name playing gargantuan tunes in a towering style suitable for grand opera, then cuts an LP using almost nothing but an acoustic guitar and harmonica, that is authentic news." In *Rolling Stone,* Steve Pond would say it loud: "This is the bravest of Springsteen's six records; it's also his most startling, direct and chilling."

Joel Selvin's review for the *San Francisco Chronicle* was stirring: "On this record, Springsteen fouls up time and meter on frequent occasion, mumbles inarticulate lyrics at points, and generally includes stray marks and moments of human fallibility anybody else would have taken the time to record over. Not that Springsteen is lazy, but, rather, the obvious intention of this work is to let the listener in on the creative process at a tender, fragile moment that can never be recaptured. . . . Never before has a major recording artist made himself so vulnerable and open."

Of course, that wasn't Springsteen's most immediate intention. If he let the listener in on the creative process, opened a private door, that wasn't his goal. It was, however, a beautiful thing that happened along the way. And Selvin was right to celebrate that act. It *wasn't* something major artists were doing.

CHAPTER SEVENTEEN

The Word on the Streets

I remember I had a friend, a neighbor, and he worked at a
record store. He said, "Oh, you like *Nebraska*?" And he put
a Jimmie Rodgers record in my hand. I think I still have it.
If you're the guy in your neighborhood who's into *Nebraska,*
things are going to come to you.

—CHUCK PROPHET, in conversation with the author

On Saturday, September 25, 1982, the Blasters played the Peppermint Lounge in New York City. The Peppermint Lounge had a history that extended back to 1958. Mafia ties linked the place to Umbertos Clam House, while the twist craze of the early 1960s gave the venue and its house band, Joey Dee and the Starliters, an audience that included Sinatra, Marilyn Monroe, Liberace, and Truman Capote. After changing its name and reopening as a gay nightclub, in 1980 the Peppermint Lounge reopened again under its original name, if in a new location with new people running the place.

The room was packed the night the Blasters played. The club was having a hot streak. Just the week before Bruce Springsteen had joined Dave Edmunds onstage, in what would be one of Springsteen's limited public appearances over the next few years. It was a different city then. You could buy heroin on streets that today might be lined with six-million-dollar town houses. The night of their gig, the Blasters received a New York City welcome.

"I remember very distinctly when I first heard about *Nebraska*," the Blasters' songwriter and guitar player Dave Alvin told me. "I was staying with Scott Kempner in New York City. The Blasters' first album on Slash Records was out. We'd gotten ripped off after playing the Peppermint Lounge. All our gear was stolen. So we had a few days to kill while we tried to round up replacement gear. To save money, I stayed at Scott's." By that time, Scott Kempner's band the Dictators had split up, and he was putting together a new band. He didn't like the feeling you got when you weren't in one.

Nebraska would be coming out five days after the Blasters' gear was ripped off, but Kempner had a promo copy and was already at work telling the world. And he was starting in his living room, where Dave Alvin was sleeping. "It fucking blew my mind. Completely. With *Nebraska* I was like, 'Holy shit, where are we going with this?' I already loved this guy. But now things got even deeper."

Dave Alvin listened but had to figure out what the Blasters were going to do to finish out their tour. By the time his band got it all figured out, *Nebraska* was on the shelves. "*The Village Voice* had this full-page review of the album," Dave Alvin explained. "Scott was a huge fan. His apartment was down there in the Village, kind of a meeting place. So, between Scott and Eric Ambel and various others, that was all that was being discussed. It was, 'What's going on here, man?' Or, 'This is great, it's his greatest.' Or, 'I don't know, man. I don't know.'"

"Yeah, I thought everyone had to hear *Nebraska,*" Kempner recalled. "It embodied a guy who was not going to listen to anybody. It embodied a guy who knew exactly what he wanted to do. You could hear that there was nothing unintentional about that record. He didn't come upon any of those songs by accident. He came upon every one of those songs because they were inside of him. It wasn't like he found them anywhere else." The exchange between Scott Kempner and Dave Alvin was just one of many taking place in that moment. By the time Dave Alvin was home in Los Angeles, it was his turn.

Alvin opened the October 9, 1982, *Billboard* to look at a piece about the Blasters titled "A Hard Rockabilly Band Blasts Away at Success," and opposite the article on page 33 was a picture of Bruce Springsteen, onstage with Dave Edmunds at the Peppermint Lounge. "Star Visit," the caption said.

"That's when I gave it a real listen," Alvin said. "I put it on, and I was floored. It was everything that, as a writer, I admired. It was right there. The brevity, and Springsteen's ability to convey a lot despite that brevity, was striking. It was a different side of his mastery. He'd already shown himself to be a master wordsmith with songs that had much more density. Now he showed just how complete a scene and a character he could develop with remarkable economy. I was in awe."

So much that was known about Springsteen, so much about him that had been celebrated was missing. The No Nukes concerts gave Springsteen a way to show what he could do with *and to* an audience. The *River* Tour had put a bandleader and his street ensemble out there, bringing rock and roll and all its theater to the people. And the shows ranked as victories, crucial to an understanding of who Bruce Springsteen is, but it was a celebration of live rock and roll at its best that illuminated some of Springsteen's gifts . . . while blurring others.

"The thing about Springsteen, and, really, a lot of the really great artists, is that they get famous for something, and then it obscures some of their deepest gifts," Dave Alvin insisted. "That applies to Merle Haggard, and, in a way, it applies to Bob Dylan. With Bruce Springsteen, I think his abilities as a performer being what they are, they sometimes keep people from seeing just how great he is as a songwriter. It may sound odd, because he's obviously recognized as a songwriter. But I don't think he gets quite what he's due. When I sat with *Nebraska,* I was sitting with one hell of a songwriter."

Richard Thompson, once of Fairport Convention and just then Richard and Linda Thompson, who happened to be at the top of the *Village Voice* poll that year along with Springsteen, saw the situation in much the same light:

The thing about Springsteen for me, though, is that he's really good at everything musical he does: great writer, great singer, and great performer. Arguably, he's one of the greatest performers of the rock era. Being successful at that, going from clubs to arenas to stadiums, the music gets bigger. The music gets more bombastic. It has to, really. But because of this, I think you can lose sight of Springsteen. Seeing him in a big, over-the-top place, an arena or stadium, doing these big performances, his virtues can be missed. You can lose sight of him as the great songwriter he is. So in that way, *Nebraska* stands as his best record. I've never changed that opinion, since it came out. I think it's a courageous record.

Springsteen the writer had gotten a little lost in the forest of his other strengths. The energy and excitement, the rock and roll show of his ensemble performances, had become such an object of celebration and renown by the time of the *River* Tour that they monopolized conversations about Springsteen the artist. Okay, but why, one has to ask, did being a great live performer cause people to lose sight of what a great *songwriter* that live performer is? Being a composer, a bandleader, and a showman all in one hadn't confused anyone when it came to Duke Ellington's gifts.

Maybe it was the residue of the late 1960s and early 1970s singer-songwriter movement, when songwriting had come to be associated with the James Taylors and Joni Mitchells. Some image of the profession that was born in that time had come to dominate: a songwriter was a long-haired individual in faded jeans, surrounded by trees and melancholy, alone with a Martin guitar. But it was a false dichotomy: Las Vegas, with its glitter and over-the-top performances and costume, was on one side, Laurel Canyon on the other.

The odd result was that even an artist like James Brown, whose legacy and influence increase with every passing year, got tangled in that same split. No matter Brown's impact as a songwriter and record maker—in 1969, *Look* magazine declared Brown the "most important black person in America today"—and no matter what his songs and recordings would mean to popular music from the 1960s forward, here was an artist not inducted into the Songwriters Hall of Fame until 2000. Kris Kristofferson was inducted in 1985. Brown's show, the magnificence of those performances, the theater and the choreography and costume changes, the band that could stop with a pump of James Brown's fist—it all put him on the "show" side of things, where Springsteen would so often find himself, the result of his own unyielding performances.

And then *Nebraska* came, in which nothing was going to distract from the songwriter . . . because everything else had been removed, save for the shadowed figure on the inner sleeve.

Rosanne Cash, daughter of Johnny Cash and renowned singer-songwriter, was already a believer when in 1982 she got her hands on *Nebraska*. "I was a huge Springsteen fan," she told me. "But the second *Nebraska* came out, I just put it on repeat forever. I loved it so much. I loved the starkness of it. I loved the melancholy of it, the characters, the landscapes. I loved how it felt like Springsteen had dropped every kind of veneer—not to say that the veneer was false, because it was an element of Bruce Springsteen that we all loved—but he dropped all that to go deep into this world and these characters. He laid it all out like they were WPA photographs. Black and white. It spoke to me."

Rosanne Cash saw Springsteen the songwriter in such high relief that she felt compelled to understand *Nebraska* in literary terms. "With *Nebraska*," she said, "he's doing some writing way outside his places of familiarity. He's into really well-drawn third-person writing, as if he were Flannery O'Connor. He's jumped into a literary role in *Nebraska*. It was searing to me. It was just the imprint of those characters and the landscape, but also who *he* was in back of them as an artist."

Hearing the songs and sounds of *Nebraska*, Rosanne Cash

couldn't help but wonder, in her words, "who *he* was in back of them as an artist." But she also wondered about another artist, her father, Johnny Cash. "I sent *Nebraska* to my dad," she explained. "I said, 'This is a record you'll clearly like.' And, yeah, I was right, my dad loved *Nebraska*. It's so beautifully conceived, thoughtful. Bruce went deep. The subtlety of the relationships between people, the drama. A song like 'Highway Patrolman.' My dad ended up recording a couple songs from *Nebraska*, 'Highway Patrolman' and 'Johnny 99.'"

Johnny Cash had taken a few left turns in his own recording career, not always finding that his audience followed him. *At Folsom Prison* proved a breakthrough. *Bitter Tears* lost a few people along the way. Both mattered. As American voices, Johnny Cash and Bruce Springsteen shared some things. "To *not* pay too much attention to what's worked before," Rosanne Cash insisted, "but to keep pushing and digging and exploring and following instincts about what's next. That's the sole motivation of an artist. I can't even imagine that Bruce would have gone, 'Oh, I've got to follow up "Hungry Heart." That's a good formula, let me keep doing that.' That's not what a real artist does. In fact, that's killed a lot of people. Eventually, it's death to any authentic impulse to create art. And I don't think Springsteen would've ever fallen prey to that. So, no, in that sense *Nebraska* didn't surprise me."

Rosanne Cash was pointing toward that bigger game of sequencing, how one full album leads into the next. Only artists with long careers, and particularly those working in the album era, got to play at that level. Johnny Cash did it. Springsteen was deep in it by *Nebraska*.

"If he'd gone from *The River* with 'Hungry Heart' to *Born in the U.S.A.* and 'Dancing in the Dark,'" Rosanne Cash considered, "it could have been a diminishment. As much as I love 'Dancing in the Dark,' it would have been a narrowing. And people might have gone, 'Okay, I get who Bruce is,' and moved on. Probably not [*laughs*]. But *Nebraska* was that flag in the ground for who he really is, right before his biggest commercial success. I don't see strategy involved. It seems like the organic life of an artist to me. But that doesn't mean it didn't work like a strategy. Like I said, I was a huge fan of *Born to Run*. I was living in London in 1976, hearing that album for the first time. It was huge. I would have stuck with him anyway. But *Nebraska*? It cemented his reputation, cemented who he was as an artist. I was in for life after *Nebraska*."

When Steve Earle got some attention for his 1986 album, *Guitar Town,* it wasn't his first attempt to make music a sustainable career. It wasn't even his first major label record deal. He'd gone back and forth between his home state of Texas and Tennessee more than once. Call it the fuck–it highway, a road traveled by a few of his heroes. For *Guitar Town,* though, Earle signed with MCA, the legendary Tony Brown acting as his A&R man. Brown came out of gospel but joined Elvis Presley's band and then Emmylou Harris's, all before making his mark as a record man and producer. The MCA label head at the time was the even more legendary Jimmy Bowen, producer of Frank Sinatra, George Strait, and many more. Bowen had a long career to his name and, some would say, answered only to God.

Steve Earle's problem was that Jimmy Bowen had a Steve

Earle problem. "*Guitar Town* was out, and it was doing okay," Earle recalled. "But the label didn't want it to happen. Jimmy Bowen certainly didn't. He didn't like the record. He didn't like me. But it was out there and got really good reviews, though mostly from the rock side of things. On the country side, the first single had died in the thirties." He joined Waylon Jennings, Willie Nelson, Kris Kristofferson, Townes Van Zandt, and artists who at different times in Nashville's history would struggle to find their places in Music City. Just then, in 1986, falling between categories wasn't a plus. But in a quiet moment out in Los Angeles, there on the Sunset Strip, unbeknownst to Earle, things were about to turn around.

" 'Guitar Town' was doing okay as the second single," Earle said. "Then, around that same time, Bruce Springsteen walked into Tower Records in L.A. and bought a couple of things. He got Willy DeVille's first solo record, and he bought *Guitar Town*. A kid who worked there at Tower reported it, and it ended up in a column in *Billboard*. I sold fifty thousand records the next week and got booked all over the place. So that was it: I had a career largely because Bruce bought my record and it got into print." But it all mattered to Steve Earle for reasons beyond that. Had Sylvester Stallone picked up *Guitar Town* that day and talked about it on Johnny Carson, it wouldn't have meant the same thing.

"I'm a singer-songwriter, and I knew how good he was," Earle told me. "When Bruce's first and second records came out, I was in Houston still. There's a really famous bootleg from '74 in Houston, Liberty Hall. I was at that show. This is just to say, I was a fan from the beginning. I knew he was the guy. I knew what he was doing. I knew he was trying to be a singer-songwriter post-disco, and that required having a rock band. I was paying attention. I was a folkie, but I knew that he was a songwriter, that we had the same job." *Nebraska,* though, allowed Earle to watch Springsteen doing the job, in just the way Earle was accustomed to seeing it done by Guy Clark and Townes Van Zandt.

"There were certain songs of his that worked for me when I played them just me and one guitar," Earle recalled. "And I did some of those. When *Nebraska* comes along, well . . . I'd always wondered what Bruce Springsteen would sound like on only one guitar. That's how I started out and what I judged everything by. If you can play a song in front of people by yourself, you have a song. *Nebraska* was, all of a sudden, a Springsteen record where I could have gone out and played any of those songs anytime I wanted to. I love the whole album. I think some of his best songs are there. I thought it was brilliant."

In the wake of *Guitar Town,* the character of Earle's recordings and his approach to live performance would be filtered through his understanding of Springsteen. "He turned a room with twenty thousand people into a coffeehouse," Earle said. "I finally realized that I had it right all along, that I didn't have to change everything 'cause I was trying to front a band and trying to get on the radio. I could just do what I did in coffeehouses, and make a record to be a record." Unlike Bob Dylan, who so often seems like a species of one, too singular to model one's artistic identity on, Springsteen was an example that many could and would follow. By 1982 he'd established a territory for the singer-songwriter that was wider than the tradition had suggested.

"As a songwriter," Earle continued, "I love the fact that *Nebraska*'s songs were obviously studies, with some lyrics from one song popping up in another. It was obviously a work in progress. It was really interesting in that respect. I learned a lot about songwriting listening to that record. It sort of validated things I was doing. . . . I'm from Texas, and Texas had started cranking up to execute people around that time, and I heard a voice in Springsteen's song. The person that's talking to you in 'Nebraska'—and he does this on other records, before *Nebraska*—will often address us, or another character, as 'sir.' That's a somewhat archaic, juvenile point of view. Addressing his male elders as 'sir,' whether he actually thinks they're better than him or not, whether he actually respects them or not, that always struck me as poignant. It tells me that the character's not grown yet, he's not a fully baked human being."

The literary character of the writing, extending the possibilities beyond a first-person, confessional voice, struck Earle as well, particularly when the perspective belonged to an unlikable character. It was that Flannery O'Connor thing. "The idea of assuming a character and talking about what happened to him," Earle emphasized, "and it's not a sympathetic character— that takes some bravery. I do this in a song called 'Gettin' Tough' on my first record, which was a few years after *Nebraska*. It's nowhere near as successful, and not as dark and deep. But I don't think I would have or could have written that song—and I definitely wouldn't have written 'Billy Austin'—without 'Nebraska.'"

The effect of *Nebraska* was contingent, at least in part, on the fact that the artist who made it could have gone after the title win . . . but didn't. And many among the listeners, including other songwriters, had to consider why, because Springsteen wasn't there to tell anyone that, not just then.

———————

Where was Springsteen when these songwriters were sifting through the sand, dirt, and clay of *Nebraska*? No one was really asking that question. *Nebraska* had such a rare intimacy to it—it was a you-and-him thing—that no one thought of Springsteen as being anywhere but right there, singing those songs to them. Where he was, though, was alone. He was at a distance from his audience for the first time after a major release.

That two-way exchange of rock and roll, so central to Springsteen's experience of his art, was on hold. Since the time he was a teenager, he'd been receiving messages from the dance floor, learning to watch for them, to feel them in the floorboards. The stammers and grunts and twisted affections, the inarticulate speech of the rock and roll response: it was Springsteen's first language. He'd talk to the audience, and they'd talk back. But with *Nebraska* it was only that call to Jon Landau. "How's the album doing?"

The isolation that informed the making of *Nebraska* was doubled by Springsteen's isolation after its release. Not a lot of thought was given to how strange and even troubling the decision not to tour might be for an artist who had gotten so much from getting onstage, from looking out there for proof of life among the bodies that looked back. If they were okay, he was okay. And they were always okay. But if they were missing? So was he.

CHAPTER EIGHTEEN

Gone Missing

I think you can get to a point where nihilism, if that's the right word, is overwhelming, and the basic laws that society has set up—either religious or social laws—become meaningless. Things just get really dark. You lose those constraints, and then anything goes. The forces that set that in motion, I don't know exactly what they'd be. I think just a lot of frustration, lack of findin' somethin' that you can hold on to, lack of contact with people, you know? That's one of the most dangerous things, I think—isolation. . . . *Nebraska* was about that American isolation: what happens to people when they're alienated from their friends and their community and their government and their job. Because those are the things that keep you sane, that give meaning to life in some fashion. And if they slip away, and you start to exist in some void where the basic constraints of society are a joke, then life becomes kind of a joke. And anything can happen.

—BRUCE SPRINGSTEEN, speaking with Kurt Loder, 1984

As he was preparing *Nebraska* for release, Bruce Springsteen was also, oddly enough, finalizing the purchase of his first home. But it wasn't in Colts Neck, wasn't even in New Jersey. Neither was it in Nebraska. It was a four-bedroom place in the Hollywood Hills, a Los Angeles address with space enough for both a private life and, soon enough, a professional-grade recording setup. He bought it without ever setting foot in the place. Really, he bought the idea of a home.

The house, at 7965 Fareholm Drive, was walking distance from Hollywood Boulevard but still far enough up the hill to offer a stunning view of the city at night, jewels scattered across a desert. Given the estates in that general area, though, this residence didn't stop anyone in their tracks or find a place on the Map of the Stars' Homes. It was modest. It did have a little

Hollywood pedigree, however: 7965 Fareholm Drive was the former residence of Sidney Toler.

Sidney Toler was old Hollywood. Born in Missouri, he'd appeared on Broadway, owned and run theater companies in Maine and Nova Scotia. But, no surprise, his career wasn't made in Maine or Nova Scotia. He's best remembered for his role as the Asian American detective Charlie Chan in the long-running film series of the same name. Toler wasn't the first person to go out to Hollywood to become someone he wasn't. And Bruce Springsteen wouldn't be the last. New house, new beginning, new man. Or so the dream went.

California was hardly an arbitrary choice for Springsteen's first experience of home ownership. His parents had moved west from New Jersey when he was a young musician stumbling toward his first recording contract, and by the late 1970s, with several tours behind him, he knew Los Angeles well. Along with New York City, L.A. was the tour stop that mattered the most for national acts. It was also a steady contrast to the sometimes harsh weather back east. Palm trees, blue skies, sand, and ocean: nature collaborated in creating perfect conditions for diminished introspection. It didn't take long for touring musicians to have favorite restaurants, know the way to the water, understand the city's traffic patterns, and, finally, talk about moving there. To wake up and see the sun, day after day after day after day.

When Springsteen made that call to Landau to see how *Nebraska* was faring, it was from the road, in the midst of a trip west to move into Charlie Chan's old place. He was on the journey with his friend Matt Delia, the same friend Springsteen mentioned years before in his *King Biscuit Flower Hour* interview. They'd tracked a route that took them not directly west but first to a few places that mattered, Memphis and New Orleans, capital cities of American music.

They drove in a 1969 Ford XL, an automobile celebrated among the vintage car crowd as Ford's largest performance car. Springsteen took it upon himself to make tapes that reflected the regions they were in. When Professor Longhair was playing over the car's speakers, you knew you were in New Orleans or getting close. Springsteen's was a studious approach to the great American road trip.

It wasn't Springsteen's first road trip, but when he published his 2016 memoir, none of the others got anything close to the space reserved for that 1982 journey. After that one, things weren't going to be the same again for Bruce Springsteen. But the story wouldn't be told in full until he was the one to tell it. "I made [*Nebraska*]," he explained to Dave Marsh for the author's 1987 biography, *Glory Days,* "it came out, I got in the car, I drove across the country, I might have been recognized once someplace or somethin'. And I was really happy with the record, I really felt that it was my best record to that date as far as an entire album goes. I felt that it was my best writing, I felt that I was getting better as a writer. I was learning things. I was certainly taking a hard look at everything around me."

But the story would change dramatically over the years. Springsteen's conversation with Marsh revealed little of what would be shared decades later. Even Marsh, talking with Peter Ames Carlin more than twenty years after the publication of *Glory Days,* addressed the matter very differently. "[Bruce] def-

initely had a major psychological crisis right about that time. . . .
I could've been clearer in the book, but wasn't because I wasn't
comfortable with it at the time. But I felt comfortable with his
depths to say the guy in 'Nebraska' isn't Charlie Starkweather.
It's him."

Only with the publication of his memoir, *Born to Run*,
would Springsteen give his audience the more unsettling, un-
filtered version of the trip west with Delia. It is, in fact, the
memoir's centerpiece. And while Springsteen has long had a
reputation as a public figure who allows his audience a view of
his private self, the story of the road trip, as Springsteen tells it,
is the man at his most unguarded.

In Springsteen's recollection, he and Delia had driven
through the South and were coming into the vast midwestern
and western landscapes of prairie and plain, when a rupture
took place within him. By that time in the trip, the end of the
journey, its inevitability, had begun to breathe on Springsteen.
Eventually the Ford XL was going to be approaching an ocean.
Then it would be a matter of turning left, turning right, turning back, or, as planned, stopping. His arrival at a new home, a
new beginning in the Hollywood Hills, was becoming an anxious matter. Memphis and New Orleans had been distractions,
and the comfort of that first leg was gone.

When the two travelers entered a small western town, coming upon a local fair, where townsfolk mixed with one another
and music played, something inside Springsteen was triggered.
He describes it in *Born to Run:*

From nowhere, a despair overcomes me; I feel an envy of
these men and women and their late-summer ritual, the

small pleasures that bind them and this town together. . . .
Right now, all I can think of is that I want to be amongst
them, of them, and I know I can't. I can only watch. That's
what I do. I watch . . . and I record. I do not engage, and if
and when I do, my terms are so stringent, they suck the
lifeblood and possibility out of any good thing, and real
thing, I might have. It's here, in this little river town, that
my life as an observer, an actor staying cautiously and safely
out of the emotional fray, away from the consequences, the
normal messiness of living and loving, reveals its cost to me.
At thirty-two, in the middle of the USA, on this night, I've
just exceeded the once-surefire soul-and-mind-numbing
power of my rock 'n' roll meds. . . . I feel a deeper anxiety
than I've ever known. Why here? Why tonight? Thirty-
four years later, I still don't know why.

"All I do know," he goes on to write, "is as we age the
weight of our unsorted baggage becomes heavier . . . much
heavier." But that *wasn't* all he knew. By the end of that passage
he moves in on the more formidable truth: "Long ago, the
defenses I built to withstand the stress of my childhood, to save
what I had of myself, outlived their usefulness. . . . Now the bill
collector is knocking, and his payment'll be in tears."

Springsteen was clear, adamant, when he told me that *Nebraska* is about his childhood, about mining those early experiences, going back there to confront his past. The *Nebraska*
songs are intimately connected with the "unsorted baggage" he
describes as getting "heavier . . . much heavier" upon entering
his thirties. And if in the past his "rock 'n' roll meds," administered nightly when he took the stage and got a much-needed

sense of connection, camaraderie, and sheer motion, allowed him to navigate adult life *despite* that baggage, in the months after *Nebraska*'s release he didn't have a hundred tour stops to dull the pain. He was moving into a new home, the first he'd ever purchased, alone, preparing to start a new life . . . with far fewer resources than he'd ever had to work with.

By the time Dave Marsh spoke to *The New Yorker*'s David Remnick in 2012, after the Peter Ames Carlin interview referenced earlier, he discussed Springsteen's mental health after the release of *Nebraska* with even less equivocation: "[Bruce] was feeling suicidal. The depression wasn't shocking, per se. He was on a rocket ride, from nothing to something, and now you are getting your ass kissed day and night. You might start to have some inner conflicts about your real self-worth." Less equivocation, yes, but not yet anything in the way of satisfying explanation—ass-kissing and rocket rides don't explain thoughts of suicide.

"Despair" is the word Springsteen uses in his memoir. When he got to Los Angeles, walking in the door of his new home, he wanted to leave immediately, to just start driving again. But to where? Every road trip, every tour, was going to end, and the endings were getting harder.

It was "Mr. Landau" whom Springsteen called, to tell him that something was not right, not right at all. The last call to Jon Landau had been to check on *Nebraska*'s chart position, but this was another kind of communication altogether. Landau had come to know when it was a manager that was needed and when it was a friend. And Landau said, simply but directly, "You need professional help." That statement wasn't casual, and it had been waiting for its moment. It was Landau who, describing to me his first listens to the *Nebraska* demos, said, they "concerned [him] on a friendship level."

It wasn't the first time the two men had talked about Springsteen's depression, but it was the first time they spoke of it as a crisis to be addressed immediately. The *Nebraska* experience was clinging to Springsteen like some kind of psychic residue. It got in the car with him as he headed for Los Angeles and met him at the door when he arrived. His account in *Born to Run* captures the state he found himself in upon arrival in L.A.:

> I've broached these subjects in several long semianalytical conversations with Jon [Landau] in the past. He gets the drift. It's dark and getting darker. My well of emotion is no longer being channeled and safely pipelined to the surface. There's been an "event," and my depression is spewing like an oil spill all over the beautiful turquoise-green gulf of my carefully planned and controlled existence. Its black sludge is threatening to smother every last living part of me. . . . At my request he makes a call, I get a number and two days later I drive fifteen minutes west to a residential home/office in a suburb of Los Angeles. I walk in; look into the eyes of a kindly, white-haired, mustached complete stranger; sit down; and burst into tears.

That's where Springsteen was when his fellow songwriters were admiring his latest recording. "There was *Nebraska*," Springsteen told me as we sat together in Colts Neck, "and then there was this breakdown. So, yeah, it makes sense that you'd connect the two."

———————

WZ: When you write a song, you inhabit the world of that song. With *Nebraska,* you'd just gone into a collection of songs that took you into your childhood. You were spending a lot of time in the trouble back there. Then things come apart.

SPRINGSTEEN: I don't know. That's a puzzle to me. You would just look at it on the surface and say, yeah, there was *Nebraska* and then there was this . . . what happened to me on that road trip. That makes sense. And that's why *Born in the U.S.A.* wasn't completed for another year or two. Once I'd gotten over the curve of where I was emotionally, I had to get to the other side of that to finish that other record. So you would look and say, very strange. [*Pause.*] I finished *Nebraska,* I took a big road trip, the road trip was just, well, an epiphany of its own, which I never really came back from. So it's a pivotal album, yes. How much your music has to do with your emotional life, I would say that I'm uncertain about that—I've written so many kinds of songs, in so many different emotional spaces, I'm not sure how they connect or even if they do connect. I'm a little hesitant to make that immediate connection.

WZ: To make it causal?

SPRINGSTEEN: I'm just not sure that that's the way creativity works and functions. [*Pauses.*] But you did have to put

yourself in that isolated place to make that record. My
hometown is ten minutes to the west. I did and still do a
lot of living there. I go back and plumb those mysteries
to this day.

WZ: And *Nebraska,* as you describe it, was a return specifi-
cally to childhood, to childhood trauma. That's a trig-
gering place, for anyone who might have that in their
past. With those songs, you went there and stayed for
some time. You moved back in.

SPRINGSTEEN: Yeah, I would say that that's true. And obviously that's what's going to happen if you're going to go
into that past the way I did. You know? I think it was
the first time, pre-analysis, of a deeply investigative period of my life, where I started to question what's the
matter with me. Something's wrong, something's not
right, I'm having a really hard time placing myself in
this world. That was the first thing that came out.
That record was the first thing that came out when
I started to go back and question my own sense of
place, who I was, what I was doing, where I came from,
that was the music that came out. And then the road
trip.

In order to write about other people's isolation, Springsteen
had gone all the way into his own. And then, having created
the document of his isolation in the form of an album called
Nebraska, for the first time he was cut off from the audience
that had always been there to provide the energy and life he fed

on. The critic and writer Robert Palmer remarked of *Nebraska*, "It's been a long time since a mainstream rock star made an album that asks such tough questions and refuses to settle for easy answers—let alone an album suggesting that perhaps there *are* no answers."

CHAPTER NINETEEN

Follow That Dream (Wherever That Dream May Lead)

Mae [Boren Axton]: You know, what I can't understand is
how you keep that leg shaking just at the right [general
laughter] tempo all the time you're singing.

Elvis: Well, it gets hard sometimes. I have to stop and rest
it—but it just automatically wiggles like that.

—from a 1955 interview reprinted in Peter
Guralnick's *Last Train to Memphis*

The time between Jon Landau's urging that Springsteen get "professional help" and the release of *Born in the U.S.A.* is something of a blur if not close to a blank in the existing accounts of Springsteen's life, even in his own memoir. It's a period in which the documentation gets thinner, the witnesses fewer.

Springsteen was in Los Angeles for the winter after his drive west and then returned to New Jersey, not getting a lot of songwriting done in either case. He was spotted at a Prince concert, already showing the effects of a new weight training routine. He was known to have returned home for Steven Van Zandt's New Year's Eve 1982 wedding, at which he joined various E Street Band members, Southside Johnny, Gary U.S. Bonds, and others for songs including "Save the Last Dance for Me,"

"Jole Blon," and "Shout." Little Richard conducted the Van Zandts' ceremony, Percy Sledge performed "When a Man Loves a Woman" as the couple came down the aisle, and Springsteen showed up without a date. But mostly it was just sightings in that period. Hollywood's Club Lingerie, joining Jimmy and the Mustangs for "Twist and Shout." A brief onstage appearance with Clarence Clemons and the Red Bank Rockers at the Keystone in Palo Alto.

Earlier in the year, when he was still in the Colts Neck rental and *Nebraska* was recorded but not completed, Springsteen would often drop by the Stone Pony in Asbury Park and join the house band. But that was a just-down-the-road, jump-onstage thing in the old neighborhood. Los Angeles was another matter. After the road trip west, Springsteen wasn't thinking about playing "Midnight Hour" for surprised club goers. Mostly he was at home, trying to make it into a place he belonged, or himself into a person who belonged there.

When Jon Landau flew out to Los Angeles the winter after Springsteen's arrival at 7965 Fareholm Drive, no one was entirely sure what was going on, Landau included. Chuck Plotkin was just *one* person who worried that, maybe, something had soured in his relationship with Springsteen. He just didn't know what. Their communication was down to a trickle.

Looking back on the situation, Plotkin suggests that Landau might have been the only one with the necessary sensitivity to understand what Springsteen was wrestling with, or at least the only one in the inner circle who could make room for Springsteen to do whatever wrestling he needed and in his own time. "Jon is the one utterly permanent and irreplaceable constant,"

Plotkin insists. "In Bruce's career, but also in his life. Jon has, over and over again, figured out how to provide the buoyancy that Bruce needs from his closest ally. Across these strange changes. I mean, when I talk to Jon about them, they don't even seem strange to him."

When it came to finally deciding to release his rough home demos as *Nebraska,* it was Springsteen alone who made the decision—but Landau was the collaborator who gave him space to do so, the one who wasn't threatened when some room *had* to open up between them. "The people around you can only take you so far," said Landau. "In that instance he'd been taken as far as we could take him."

Managing Springsteen, as Landau had come to practice it, was an art of intuition, of knowing when to step back as much as when to step in. With Springsteen in Los Angeles, in the wake of that breakdown, Landau wasn't going to push his artist into making *Nebraska*'s follow-up . . . no matter that Landau felt they were sitting on the makings of a remarkable album. "Born in the U.S.A.," "Glory Days," "My Hometown," "Cover Me," and the other recordings were still on the shelf.

"I had my own ambitions as producer and manager," Landau told me. "I wanted this thing to succeed. I had tremendous pride in what we had done. And I knew this was the moment. I had my own sense for what he had to do in this moment. He was a person with incredible influence at that time." Landau could feel an alignment, the possibility of a crowning experience that was the result of years of momentum. He was only lacking one key element: Bruce Springsteen.

"He was so introspective," Landau said. "I'm not talking

about the psychotherapy; he was introspective long before the psychotherapy. I'm talking about since I'd known him. Everything for him was a matter of identity. His fears about *if* he became so big, would it invalidate or contradict his identity as an artist? Would he become a pop star and have people lose the focus on his deepest talent? I just had confidence that this moment was meant to be, that it's part of the story. And *Nebraska* was part of that story, too." But Landau wasn't saying any of that to Springsteen just then. Landau was listening.

There were certainly a few people around Springsteen eager to supply ideas of what *they* felt should happen next, but Springsteen wasn't facing a shortage of ideas. That would never be his dilemma, not then and not now. His well-documented deliberation and second-guessing, which informed the making of several of his best-known albums, *Born to Run* and *Darkness on the Edge of Town* among them, were part of a creative process, not some sign that he'd run out of ideas.

If anything, abundance was the problem when there was one, having to choose from all that was there. Landau had discovered early that managing Springsteen had far more to do with timing than generating ideas. He'd learned to trust that Springsteen was on a path, even if that path was, in some sections, unmarked. In fact, Landau often protected Springsteen's right to get lost.

Landau wasn't yet Springsteen's manager when he first recognized that the rhythms of the creative work were most commonly the thing he could help with. Stopping and starting. With Springsteen in the middle of *Born to Run* and in too deep to see where he was in relation to the whole, Landau told him that *Born to Run* was, in Landau's view, a finished recording. It could be over, Landau suggested, but it would have to be Springsteen's choice to end it. He saw an artist at risk of trying to make a recording that said everything that could ever be said. There's a point, Landau told his friend and co-producer, when you're working on an album so long that you're in danger of going into its follow-up. Just then, Springsteen was ready to hear those words, and he let the process stop.

Heading to meet Springsteen at his new Los Angeles home in 1983, Landau had some sense that with *Born in the U.S.A.* the timing was going to be about when to encourage Springsteen to see that, as Landau put it, "this was the moment." But when he got to Springsteen's house, Landau knew his own timing was off. "Bruce played me some things, great stuff, of course," he recalled to me. "But I saw that we were back to the drawing board."

"How," Chuck Plotkin asked, considering Landau's style, "is it possible to be as supportive as you need to be and still be an honest critic of the work? Striking that balance likely sounds easier than it is. Jon is not a yes-man, but he has a great capacity to know when to be what for Bruce." Listening to Springsteen's new recordings at the Fareholm Drive house, neither Landau nor Springsteen knew exactly where they stood.

—

"The plan," Dave Marsh writes in *Glory Days,* "was for Bruce to come to California and spend several weeks mixing the rock and roll material with Plotkin. At the same time, Bruce arranged for Toby Scott to install a more elaborate twenty-four-track home studio in an outbuilding at his Los Angeles home. But it wasn't quite that easy to change gears from the gloomy and insulated world of *Nebraska* to the more open and friendly space of *Born in the U.S.A.*"

"He had a little two-car garage, and over it was an apartment," recalled Toby Scott. "I said, 'Yeah, I'll get you set up.' I put together a little recording studio, made up of a Trident Trimix console of, I believe eight, twelve channels, maybe even sixteen, and an eight-track MCI tape machine, one-inch tape. I added a cheap Orban spring reverb. I was never into spending a lot of money. Then I taught Mike [Batlan] how to record. Mike took notes. He recorded about a half a dozen songs on eight-track." What Springsteen wasn't doing, though, was "mixing the rock and roll material."

With the Fareholm Drive studio installed and Batlan acting as engineer, Springsteen would, in stops and starts, work on some music. "County Fair" comes from that period, and in the wake of Springsteen's memoir it's hard not to see the song in the light of the depression that descended on him toward the end of that road trip. In that small town in the west he came upon a local scene that seemed to him bucolic and out of his reach. "County Fair" captures the world he couldn't be a part of, an idealized picture of community, connection, small-town peace. It's the antithesis of *Nebraska*'s hopelessness.

"He wanted crickets on that one ["County Fair"]. There were crickets up there on the side of the hill. I said, 'Go up there with a mic, use one of the condenser mics, and put it out there and crank the volume way up. You'll get the sound of crickets.' So he did that. Bruce knew we had the equipment. It was different from using a TEAC four-track, for sure. He mixed to a Sony F1, a kind of digital prototype. It used VHS or Beta. It was far from what we dealt with for *Nebraska*."

What wasn't different was the man alone, without a band behind him. But the sound and the feel and the sentiment of the Fareholm Drive recordings were already a departure from the *Nebraska* recordings, if an uncertain departure. There was a lack of cohesion to the songs that emerged in that time; they pulled in different directions. "County Fair" is a mid-tempo song, played to a drum machine, with synthesizer pads sweetening the track. It leans toward what would be coming with *Tunnel of Love*. Springsteen's voice certainly doesn't need to fight its way through the thicket of a rock and roll combo.

"Richfield Whistle," another from that time, is one that could almost have fit on *Nebraska* were it not for the story resolving with a kind of moral closure. A man has a choice to step back from violence and crime, to return to his wife and the love that's possible there, despite the unforgiving working life in which he's caught. And he chooses home. In a similar way, "The Klansman" has a strong sense of right and wrong in its story. There's no room to identify with the man selling white supremacy. Springsteen didn't do for the Klansman what he did for Charles Starkweather. The songs that were coming didn't connect one to the next in the way of the Colts Neck material. But it would be a mistake to make too much of that. The search for direction is often how records are found.

Though the mostly empty rooms of Springsteen's house were slowly getting furnished, the place remained foreign to him, a hotel without a front desk. By installing a home studio as quickly as he had, Springsteen decorated his life with transitions, personally, musically, psychologically. The messy in-betweens are often what's hidden from view as a recording artist's life and work are organized in bins, release by release. The struggle to create, the waiting, the stops and starts of song-writing, the setting off in one direction only to have to back-track, the unkind words spoken under pressure, the empty hours waiting on a song: all are mostly obscured. Those record bins are finally a distorted lens through which to consider a hu-man's trajectory. Monotony and grocery shopping are among the hidden secrets of the record maker's life.

Two recordings in particular shed light on Springsteen's whereabouts as he made his way from *Nebraska* to *Born in the U.S.A.*: "Johnny Bye Bye," which had been recorded once be-fore, in the *Nebraska* sessions, and "Follow That Dream." These are the hinge songs he needed to spend time inside so that he could find his way forward. The first was a dramatic reworking of Chuck Berry's "Bye Bye Johnny," credited to Springsteen/ Berry, the second a cover of an Elvis Presley cut. Normally, when Springsteen did other people's material, it was in the context of the live shows, not studio recordings. It was an odd but telling situation: Springsteen was concealing himself be-hind other people's writing.

So many years later, when he sat down with me, Springsteen contrasted the profound visibility of *Born in the U.S.A.* with the shadows in which he worked on *Nebraska,* talking about how the one made the other possible. "Because of *Nebraska,*" he told me, "I could go as far in the other direction as I wanted to go. Which I did. And that'd be fine, it would be fine. *Nebraska* gave me a lot of freedom. It gave me a lot of creative freedom. I don't know if there would have been a *Born in the U.S.A.* in the form it was in without *Nebraska* being released in front of it. So those two records do have a symbiotic relationship. They occurred at the same time. Those records were recorded simultaneously. Enough to where I thought they were one record at one moment. That's how connected they are."

While connected, bound to each other, the albums were like two sides of the man, the extremes of Springsteen's career and character. He'd been almost missing, and then he would come out of hiding into a kind of light brighter than anything he'd experienced in his career. The near anonymity of *Nebraska* and the almost heroic presence of *Born in the U.S.A.* reminded me, I told him, of another "odyssey," borrowing his word for the self-investigation that was beginning in the Fareholm Drive period. He allowed me to see this one through.

WZ: In Homer's *Odyssey,* the hero recovers his place as a husband and father, finds his home, but only by reentering that home, after twenty years away, disguised as a beggar, anonymous, stripped of his former glories [*pause*].

SPRINGSTEEN: Go on.

WZ: After war, misadventure, temptation, struggles of ego and lust, various trials, Odysseus returns to Ithaca, his true home, but the place is filled with suitors, men who want his wife's hand and control of his household. He can't simply announce himself; he's far outnumbered and would be slaughtered. So he returns disguised as a beggar. Meaning, Odysseus can only recover his position by first being nobody, Nobody, which he failed to do at the outset of his journey in a fit of hubris after escaping the Cyclops. So Odysseus learns from that earlier display of hubris and allows the suitors to treat him as nothing, a beggar in his own home, as an almost invisible man. But his power comes from exactly this, the relinquishing. From that position, he kills off the suitors who have taken his home. The point being that the only way to restore his place as man and hero was to first be nobody.

SPRINGSTEEN: Incredible.

WZ: I can't help but look at *Nebraska,* leading into *Born in the U.S.A.,* as part of an artistic trajectory that somehow aligns with this. *Nebraska* sets it all aside, all the glory and achievement, the studio gloss, the big sounds, the band, the picture of a hero on the front cover, the interviews in which you tell the tales of your travels. It's all set aside. The recordings are loose, muddy at times, unfinished. And then you return, with *Born in the U.S.A.,* with all the heroic trappings. But, like Odysseus, to get to the one, the heroic, you first have to give all that up. That's *Nebraska.* For me, the entire scope of your career, everything, fits between these two projects.

SPRINGSTEEN: It does. To this day. My perimeters were set in that moment.

WZ: In your book you actually use the word "odyssey," saying that between those two recordings was the beginning of your personal odyssey.

SPRINGSTEEN: I know that with *Nebraska* I was interested in

making myself as invisible as possible. I just wanted to be
another ghost. On that particular record. It spoke to
some need in me. Some roaring need. That might have
been a result of having had the kind of success that I
had. But I needed to know that I could go back and be
nobody. If I really needed to. It was an interesting moment. And, yes, then *Born in the U.S.A.* became possible.

Jon Landau has his own way of talking about what the albums meant in relation to each other. "The *Nebraska* album—
and this is not why it exists, that's not the point—but the
Nebraska album," he told me, "made the *Born in the U.S.A.*
album possible." He continued:

One of the things that figures in to that sequencing idea is
that Bruce—and forgive me for playing the psychiatrist
here—but Bruce had a dream that was about big success.
He obviously wanted it because . . . I have a theory about
this, that nobody becomes a big success unless they want to
become a big success. It just doesn't happen by accident.
For anybody. And if it does, it doesn't last for fifty years.
You can accidentally have a big hit. You can't accidentally
have a superstar career. Bruce knew inside that he had the
potential to be just about as big as he wanted to be. And he
also had another side which really questioned the value of
that and whether or not that was even something that was
morally correct and whether or not any thinking guy could
compromise his own, inner integrity to go after that. I
think *Nebraska* was liberating. Because he was so proud of

that record. He'd made as uncommercial a statement as it was possible to make relative to who he was. It was so clear as a turn away from what he'd established, even by the early '80s.

The albums were going to be two ways of answering the same question, a question that Springsteen had turned over in his mind many times: *Should I really go after the big success?* He answered "no" with *Nebraska,* and then he answered "yes" with *Born in the U.S.A.* Both answers were correct. But there he was, in Los Angeles, in between those two responses to a question upon which, it seems, a significant part of his identity hinged. And that's where and why "Johnny Bye Bye" and "Follow That Dream" mattered just a little more than the other songs he was recording in that same period.

"Johnny Bye Bye" and "Follow That Dream" were songs that allowed Springsteen to linger on the idea of Elvis Presley, as myth, symbol, and man. Presley had given Springsteen the desire to be a performer, and a model for what it looked like. But Presley's success came so fast and took on such unprecedented proportions that Presley never had a chance to ask himself the question, "Should I really go after the big success?"

When Springsteen played "Follow That Dream" and "Johnny Bye Bye" on the *River* Tour in 1980–81, he would sometimes speak of Elvis to his audience. "I remember," Springsteen said one night, "when a friend of mine called to tell me that [Presley] had died. It was so hard to understand how somebody whose music came in and took away so many people's loneliness and gave so many people a reason and a sense of the possibilities of living could have, in the end, died so tragically." It was a moving setup that, on that night, led into Springsteen's much-altered version of "Follow That Dream."

Elvis's original "Follow That Dream" was recorded for the 1962 film of the same name. It wasn't an obvious Elvis cover, nothing rock and rollers went out of their way to find. It wasn't the Sun Records Elvis of "That's All Right" or anything like the "Hound Dog" he cut for RCA. With lines like "When your heart gets weary, time to sing a song," it was closer to the territory of golden age musicals than early rock and roll. But Springsteen dropped the tempo and rewrote what lyrics he needed to, including the above-mentioned line. There was a longing in Springsteen's version unknown to Presley's original.

If you were in that audience when Springsteen spoke of Elvis and all you ever knew of the "King of Rock and Roll" were the cartoonish imitators and the superstar's tabloid-fodder final days, Springsteen's sense of loss and sorrow might have seemed misallocated. But Springsteen had a perspective on Elvis common enough among those who experienced Presley's emergence, when the legend was not yet a legend. Everyone has their "genesis moment," Springsteen would later say in a SXSW keynote. "Mine was 1956."

Elvis on *The Ed Sullivan Show*. It was the evening I realized a white man could make magic, that you did not have to be constrained by your upbringing, by the way you looked, or by the social context that oppressed you. You could call upon your own powers of imagination. You could create a transformative self, a certain type of transformative self that perhaps at any other moment in American history might have seemed difficult if not impossible.

Springsteen got a direct message that night in 1956. The "transformative self," as an idea, meant that you could get the hell out of there, whatever your "there" was, psychological, physical, or both. By sheer intuition, Springsteen, still a child at the time, knew this mattered. He wouldn't need to be "constrained" by the living room in which he found himself, there under a portrait of his deceased aunt.

At the time of those first *Ed Sullivan Show* appearances, that kind of empowering message wasn't handed to young people with any kind of regularity. The anxious talk around juvenile delinquency was focused on *harnessing* transformations among young people, on keeping them from becoming creatures that couldn't be controlled. Elvis was a vision of liberation, even triumph, there for the minds, hearts, and imaginations of young Americans. Springsteen heard the call at a very young age.

Yes, it would be hard for later generations—meaning, those who first saw Elvis as a thing of decline and decay—to fully grasp what happened for Springsteen and others who discovered Elvis in the mid-1950s. On some level, you had to be there then, and better still if you needed the message. The relentless packaging of Elvis, as records, movies, a body and face made into a commodity, which began almost immediately after his first commercial success, would make it difficult, and eventually impossible, to look back and see Elvis as had his early audiences. Johnny Rotten of the Sex Pistols would respond to Presley's death saying, "Fuckin' good riddance to bad rubbish."

Where, Springsteen wondered aloud on the *River* Tour, did all the promise of Elvis circa 1956 go? By his death, Presley's "transformative self" had become not a symbol of possibility but a cautionary tale, a transformation that found a man lost to himself. What had gone wrong, and when? Elvis, or Johnny Cash, or Bo Diddley, or Carl Perkins, or James Brown: they were people who understood what it was like to be very poor. And because of their successes they looked back on childhood poverty from a high and distant place. Yet, somehow, you knew what they came from—no matter the gold and the glitter coming off the stage. They were all, in their different ways, transformative selves.

You could look through the 1954 yearbook of any New England prep school or Ivy League university and not run into a single Elvis Presley. At the time of his emergence, Elvis wasn't the name, or the face, or the look, or the style of privilege. He signified, in a clear and consistent manner, working-class identity. He was a shitkicker, and you could tell just by looking at him. Elvis's famous gold lamé suit, made by Nudie's of Hollywood, didn't mask the truck driver; it elevated the truck driver.

He rose spectacularly. But his end? His end would suggest that what might start as an American dream can become a deal gone very wrong.

Springsteen's ambivalence about his own success was in many ways borne out by Presley's example. But to move ahead in his own career, he needed to believe it could be otherwise. Presley's end need not be his own. "Johnny Bye Bye" concludes with the clearest statement of his feelings regarding a hero's final days: "You didn't have to die / You didn't have to die." Rock and roll had sent some very poor kids into magnificent worlds, as Springsteen knew well, but no amount of Cadillacs could remove poverty's mark. Springsteen, it seems, would struggle to do as his hero hadn't and would stay close to his roots. His obsessive trips to Freehold, driving past the dilapidated homes he knew as a boy, were the practice that came of that theory. He knew that Gracelands were places of deception.

But Springsteen also knew he was going to go after the big success. He understood both things. It was a matter of readying himself, of doing it differently. First it would be *Nebraska,* invisibility. Then the time he spent in those songs, "Johnny Bye Bye" and "Follow That Dream," like mediations, preparing him for what was coming next. He was lifting weights, searching, singing to Elvis, unconsciously preparing for something he surely felt coming.

"My father didn't really survive, except in the most basic ways," Springsteen said, sitting across from me. "So I was really the first one to sort of escape that whole . . . my sister did in her own way. With the life of my parents, though . . . Jesus. Yeah, my life is another life." More success was only going to take him further away from where he came from. But out there in Los Angeles he was making the ropes that would keep him tied down to the earth.

SPRINGSTEEN: To me, *Born in the U.S.A.* was just what I had. That's all. It was just what I had available for songs.

That was what I put on that record. I went through everything, took a long, long time. I waited a year just to get "Bobby Jean." "Dancing in the Dark" Jon forced me into. It's so funny, I put together the best pieces I had, and we put the record out.

WZ: On the receiving end it felt like a statement, and I listened to it that way.

SPRINGSTEEN: Funny. So did a lot of other people, I guess. But, for me, that was my experience. I just put together what seemed like the best stuff I had.

Jon Landau walked in the door at Fareholm Drive to find a Bruce Springsteen who was in the in-betweens. In between his New Jersey rentals and the first home he'd ever purchased. In between his life in a band and a solo adventure. In between his last romantic relationship and whatever was coming next. In between *Nebraska* and a record that remained unknown, even if it was sitting right there. In between his present and a past that had been reawakened. When that first little bit of music started to come, it would have to make its way through all that in-betweenness. "The Drawing Board" is what Landau called the place. None of the music Springsteen wrote and recorded in that time was going to appear on his next album; it would just take a bit of time to understand that.

Jon Landau wasn't telling Springsteen to return his attention to the tracks that had been recorded at the Power Station. He wasn't talking about hits, asking for "Dancing in the Dark." He wasn't even asking Springsteen to please not make *Nebraska II*. He was just going to see his friend, to get a sense for where he was at. They talked about Elvis, books, some movies, art, where they'd have lunch. In time, Landau would help build a delicate bridge back to the idea of a big album. But not then.

The big album would be so big that it would obscure the many months of uncertainty that followed the earlier *Nebraska*. The sheer power with which *Born in the U.S.A.* came into the world, more a detonation than a release, was like nothing Springsteen or his fans had ever seen. Everything he'd created earlier in his career and everything that came after would be organized in relation to *Born in the U.S.A.* It didn't matter what Springsteen told the world: people were going to see *Born in the U.S.A.* as the result of great intention and strategy, as if he'd had it in his mind for years. The artist ambivalent about hit singles was not going to have much of a vote with *Born in the U.S.A.;* the album itself would take over.

The CBS executive Al Teller, the man who had seen *Nebraska* as a work of poetry that needed delicate, appropriate promotion in the marketplace, would have a different thing to contend with when he was handed the follow-up. "Next we gave him *Born in the U.S.A.,*" Jon Landau recalled, "which is his bread and butter. Top 40. Seven top ten singles. He was just . . . the fucking energy he had." In some cases you could have it both ways, an album-era release that also had a few singles to keep the momentum. But what Teller got was the biggest album-to-album contrast in Springsteen's career. As one insider put it, "*Born in the U.S.A.,* that was when the E Street members started buying houses."

"I didn't mind having the hit when we had it," Springsteen said when I asked him about the earlier "Hungry Heart." "I'm always a little suspicious of that stuff, and it wasn't what I was fundamentally interested in, but I didn't mind. It's just that I was an album artist. We remain so to this day. The only time we had any hits was when the album we were doing was such a hit that the songs became hits. Born in the U.S.A. That's our greatest hits record. Just put that on and play it through. But the rest of the time, we didn't have singles. We had very few popular singles." It led people to imagine that Born in the U.S.A. had some kind of master plan behind it, a battle strategy. But it didn't. It had Nebraska behind it. That's where Born in the U.S.A. got its strength.

Jon Landau's most conspicuous entrance into the process of making Born in the U.S.A. came when he pushed Springsteen to write the song that would become Born in the U.S.A.'s first single, "Dancing in the Dark." That was the final piece in the Born in the U.S.A. collection, and Springsteen was going to let it happen. The absolute refusal to make Nebraska conform to anything even close to the dominant rock aesthetic of 1982 loosened Springsteen up enough to give Landau, finally, a stronger position. Nebraska, what Springsteen referred to as "the best collection of songs I'd written," was a place Springsteen could go when he needed to remember where he came from.

CHAPTER TWENTY

On Repeat

Jimmy Iovine, a man who would experience remarkable success as an engineer and producer, who would start Interscope Records and, finally, launch Beats with Dr. Dre, started with a broom in his hands, just to get inside the door of a recording studio. Custodial work was to the recording studio what the mail room was to the talent agency. It was the unofficial point of entry into the world of commercial music. Iovine was never the type to sit back and wait for good fortune to come his way, so he took the broom and started sweeping. There's a balance to be struck between dreaming and doing. Once he'd established the dreaming, the easy part, Jimmy worked the doing like a man who knew exactly what he hoped to leave behind.

It worked. Iovine got himself into the studio with John Len-

non. Then he got himself into the studio with Bruce Springsteen and the E Street Band. There was some Meat Loaf in
there too. In the case of working with Springsteen, he did it
not from above but from below. He wasn't even an engineer
when he got on the project. He'd traded the broom for work
as a *second* engineer, the one who typically handles the coffee
machine and the tidying up as much as anything else. The second engineer is the guy coiling cables and cleaning up after the
drummer. It's the exceptional second engineers or the driven
second engineers who move over one seat to become engineers proper. And then they might have a voice in the conversation.

What does it take to make that advance? Sometimes it's a
willingness to start work at 3:00 a.m., without much warning.
Sometimes it's just a matter of being there when the other guy
leaves the room to check on the golf clubs he ordered. Jimmy
took anything he could get and, in the end, got near everything. No one is entirely clear when he went from being second engineer to an engineer. That story's a little fuzzy.

In the winter of 2008 I was at the dinner table, a marginal
figure at best, when Bruce Springsteen and Steven Van Zandt
broke bread with a few others at Jimmy's house in Beverly
Hills. Those present included Jimmy's wife at the time, Vicki,
and a gentleman then running Paramount Studios. Will.i.am
from the Black Eyed Peas came for dessert. The reason for this
gathering? Interscope, the enormously successful record label
Jimmy started after an enormously successful career producing
records, was releasing the soundtrack to Martin Scorsese's Rolling Stones documentary, *Shine a Light*. The E Street Band was

in town on the Magic Tour and had a night off. After dinner, in the Iovine's home theater, there would be a screening of the Scorsese film. But, really, at the heart of the evening was old friends having dinner. It was, I think, the first time Bruce and Steven, together, had visited Jimmy's Beverly Hills place.

Only a handful of rock stars will ever have a home like Jimmy Iovine's. The Elton Johns of the world, they have them. The real money, some would argue, is with those who sell the stuff, not those who make it. The dealers, not the growers. Jimmy got some of that selling action before streaming made the marketplace a more complicated affair. But by that time he'd already moved to headphones. In the new century, you'd have to be a pretty big artist to do a whole lot more than rent Jimmy's pool house.

But in the same way that family members regress in one another's presence, no matter the passing of decades or the successes they might have experienced, so it is with people who shared intimate work situations, such as that of making records. That night in Beverly Hills, the guys who were around for the making of *Darkness on the Edge of Town* reverted to who they were back then. Jimmy might have secured those ten acres in the Los Angeles area, but in some ways he was still the engineer who had started as a second engineer. The constellations that form between people early often change little over time. But it was Jimmy's house in Beverly Hills where the dinner took place. I don't think that was lost on anyone.

Because of the Scorsese film, the talk at the table turned to the Rolling Stones. That's when Bruce and Steven took the conversation and went someplace with it. Here were two guys who had known each other longer than anyone else at the dinner. When it came to talking about the Rolling Stones, they were as much two young men in bands with strong opinions about rock and roll as they were rock and roll legends themselves. And those strong opinions were not about the greatness of the Rolling Stones—that was a given—but about what period, what record, what contributions mattered the most and why. This was a couple of biblical scholars who were also believers hashing it out. It wasn't about converting anyone. For the most part, everyone else at the table just listened. It was probably the best show in town that night.

What stuck with me was something Springsteen said about Mick Jagger as a lyricist. It rubbed against the it's-only-rock-and-roll idea, upon which the Stones have built their legend. Springsteen, taking care to say this as if considering its full consequences, argued that Jagger's writing can be appreciated, understood in the way we appreciate and understand Bob Dylan's. At that level. My first thought, surprised by the argument, was, "Did the new Dylan really just say that about the other Dylan?" But I'd already missed the first turn in the road: He obviously hadn't said anything about Dylan. He'd only mobilized some idea of Dylan to get us to think differently of Jagger.

I never heard "(I Can't Get No) Satisfaction" in quite the same way after that dinner. Behind the legendary riff, in those words and the way those words are delivered, is a vision of identity in the postwar commercial age that's as immersed and complicated as Andy Warhol's. But it's certainly not the lone example of great writing attributed to Jagger/Richards. "Brown Sugar," "Sympathy for the Devil," "Shattered," "Midnight Rambler," "Paint It, Black."

Springsteen's argument involved reading the Stones against the grain. The band's (unwritten) manifesto might say, "It's only rock and roll, jackass, don't build a church on top of it." But, following Springsteen's example, it's our right to ignore all that. We're fans, and we get to do this. That night Springsteen was speaking as a fan, sitting next to another one, a guy with whom he'd debated rock and roll for a very long time.

How many hours had those two particular fans given to thinking about the Stones? And, obviously, the job wasn't complete and wouldn't ever be complete. They were chewing on the same bone and still getting meat off it. That, arguably, is what gives songs and recordings their greatest power—we can keep going back and getting more. The brevity of the popular song, our almost compulsive listening practices, and the very personal nature of how we take the stuff in: it all contributes to music's self-replenishing quality. The best material seems to continually allow for new meanings. Those two fans were layering one more conversation about the Stones on top of many, many others they'd had since they were adolescents.

Novels we might read twice, generally once. Movies we might see a few times. Our favorite recordings? We can listen hundreds, even thousands of times. They go through our systems in a very different way. A great recording, listened to hundreds and hundreds of times over a period of years, even decades, can suddenly open onto a new vista or back alley. The medium is dense. And, obviously, whatever one is going through in life triggers that density in different ways.

Onstage in 1990, talking to his audience and setting up *Nebraska*'s "Mansion on the Hill," Springsteen described those car rides taken with his father through Freehold, New Jersey. "We would drive around the town," he explained. "It was funny. We'd lived there. Always. But yet we'd go sightseeing." Same town, new ways of seeing it. Sightseeing in the place you know best. That's what listening to great songs and recordings is like. Some would say that the special ones are just better for sightseeing, even if you think of them as your own backyard. Songs like "(I Can't Get No) Satisfaction." You could drive past that sucker a thousand times and still come up with new ideas about what's going on in there.

Career songwriters know how people consume music because in most cases that's where it all started for them, as consumers themselves, falling in love with songs, playing them over and over. So they know that if they write a good one, someone out there will listen on repeat. For the songwriters like Springsteen, the song is *created* as a thing to be visited many times. So make it ready for the sightseers.

After decades in the world, *Nebraska* is one of those recorded works recognized for its simplicity but also for its density, its many-layeredness. It's a record you come back to, a record with more than its share of mystery, a record that keeps mattering and keeps throwing off new meanings. Maybe it's the record of Springsteen's that's the most collaborative with the listener. Unfinished. You could say he left it for us to complete. He trusted his art, and trusted us to do something with it.

EPILOGUE

Seeing the Place

A round the time this book was nearing completion, I got a call from an unknown number. It was Springsteen. "Warren," he said with some satisfaction, "I'm standing in the room where forty years ago I recorded *Nebraska*." He hadn't been there since 1982 but laughed at all that remained the same. My first question was obvious. The wall-to-wall orange shag rug, is it still there? He confirmed that it was so, safe from any heavy-handed remodeling. "If you want to see the room," he told me, "the owner said it'd be okay. We just have to find a time when the renters aren't home, and we can go out there together."

In an earlier email, when Bruce asked if there was anything else I needed for the book, I had only asked if he could share the address of the Colts Neck rental. I wanted to look at the place from the outside before I wrapped up the project. But he was going to do me one better and give me the final stop on my pilgrimage. We would be going in. I'd envisioned the room and the house so many times. Writing books is a strange, mostly solitary affair. You work from research, archival materials, testimony. You listen to voices; you hear voices. But the writing itself is still the imaginative process of a single person, looking out a window at something that isn't there. It's educated conjuring. Given this, the opportunity to finally bring a certain materiality to it all is profound. To be in that room with Springsteen, standing on the orange shag carpeting.

It was only a matter of days before I made my way out to Colts Neck, first going to Springsteen's home to meet him. I'd cleaned my younger son's hockey gear out of our Volkswagen, just in case Bruce was going to drive with me. I didn't know how it was going to go down. Arriving at the property, I drove to the same spot where I'd parked for the interviews and went to the recording studio, which has all the gear needed to make commercial recordings. As with most artists of Springsteen's caliber, there's no need for him to leave home to make records of the highest quality.

I was there for only a few minutes when a very clean blue 1970 El Camino pulled up. We wouldn't be taking the Volkswagen. "Patti got this for me after we used it in *Western Stars*," Springsteen explained. Why, I wondered aloud as we headed out the driveway, does every car of that general vintage seem to have the exact same smell? We considered this. Oil and gas leaks over time, common materials, upholstery—there's a recipe they all seem to follow that gets you to that scent. If you love cars from that era, or if you simply come from that era, it's an opening onto the past. Which, Springsteen acknowledged, was where we were going anyway.

The owner of the Colts Neck rental where *Nebraska* was made is still the owner. He's a realtor in the area. But, like many realtors, he's not just a realtor. He's got some stuff cooking on the side. That day, prior to our visit, he was meeting with a team from a Philadelphia museum there to pick up some cannons from the Revolutionary War era. The cannons, it seems, have a direct tie to George Washington. It was a major score for the museum and an already interesting day in rural New Jersey for the team when . . . a guy that looked a lot like Bruce Springsteen walked in. The collective astonishment among the cannon transport people was obvious enough. You could see them looking at each other in that is-it-just-me-or-does-that-guy-look-like-Bruce-Springsteen way. Just that quickly, the stories they thought they'd be telling about picking up George Washington's cannons became something else altogether.

Leaving the others in the living room, I followed Springsteen down a hallway and back to the bedroom where *Nebraska* was recorded. The orange wall-to-wall shag carpeting was most certainly intact, if a little washed out from the passage of time. The window that looked out onto the reservoir, once covered with drapes, was larger than what had been there in 1982. The bed was turned ninety degrees from where Springsteen had his. There were various things, including a somewhat large model of a schooner, stored there. But mostly, Springsteen confirmed, this looked like the place where it had happened.

"The bed was right there, the headboard at that side wall,"

Bruce explained, pointing things out. "In that corner of the room there was a round, antique table where we put the recording machine. Mike was there. I had a chair at the end of the bed, with the mics in front of me. That was it. That's how we made the record." There was some quiet, the two of us taking it in, then Springsteen handed me his phone and said, "Can you grab a picture of me in here?" So I took a photograph of Bruce Springsteen in a room that had once been full of trouble and songs.

The owners of the house were kind enough to lend me the only photographs I could find anywhere of the *Nebraska* house as it looked in the early 1980s. Though the bedroom where the record was recorded remains much as it was, the house had been expanded after Springsteen moved out, with a second story added, more square footage on the first floor, an expanded kitchen. The photographs they handed me were of a place that was no longer really there.

In 1982 it wasn't a given that Bruce Springsteen would be looking back over four-plus decades of life, a husband and father, the leader of a rock and roll band with most of its early members still performing at his side. But how he got that far is part of another, longer adventure story. This story, that of *Nebraska,* unfolds still, but it stopped belonging to Springsteen some time ago. Now it's in the hands of the next person who starts digging a little deeper, who wonders what this album is, the one with the black-and-white photo and the blood-red lettering.

ACKNOWLEDGMENTS

Playing in a rock and roll band brought me a lot of joy and a lot of grief. It also gave me access to key information I'd later need as a writer. In talking to my sons, I sometimes refer to the world of entertainment as "the disappointment business." It'll break your heart in a hundred ways. But, as I tell them, it'll also give you something to do with it, whether you're a songwriter, an actor, a dancer, a photographer, whatever. As I insist, that's a pretty reasonable deal relative to what's possible out there.

So my first thanks go to my old band, the Del Fuegos. Dan Zanes, Tom Lloyd, and Woody Giessmann. Together we learned a lot about human nature, about the fragility of rock and roll combos as social units, and about the lasting thrill of plugging in. The sack of stories we walked away with seems to replenish itself. There's always one more account of what happened in Buffalo, St. Louis, Tuscaloosa, and so on. The Del Fuegos gave me the background I needed for the thing I didn't yet know I was going to do.

My agent, Sloan Harris, originally came to me through Peter Guralnick, a dear friend and canny adviser. Peter assured me that Sloan would speak his mind. And, indeed, Sloan has done that, telling me "no" more than he's told me "yes." But if every "no" finds me drawing the blinds and needing some time alone, when a "yes" comes, I know it's well built. When he said he liked the idea of this *Nebraska* project, suggesting we take it to editor Gillian Blake, that was a good day. I was in Athens, Georgia, there with my son Piero, having just run a half marathon at the suggestion of another friend, Bertis Downs. I can see the hotel room I was in when Sloan gave me that "yes."

Gillian has been thinking about Bruce Springsteen for quite a while now. We talked about Bruce at length, even before this book was a reason to do so. Young when *Nebraska* came out, Gillian recalled wondering about its difference, why he released it when he did, why he released it at all. Like me, she was drawn to *Nebraska*'s strangeness. Just when everything was getting cleaner, *Nebraska* got dirty and mumbled its obsessions. She got it, and she encouraged me to go after this one. But, to her credit, Gillian also felt the subject opened onto broader questions about music making and music makers entering the digital era. That mattered to me and, I believe, to this book.

A big part of the *Nebraska* story is, of course, its lasting influence. Many of my conversations were with artists who had nothing to do with the album's making but for whom the recording symbolized some let's-tear-it-all-down-before-we-start-building spirit in which they remain invested. Among them are people I've known for some time and consider friends: Patty Griffin, Richard Thompson, Dave Alvin, Steve Earle, and Chuck Prophet. Others, like Rosanne Cash and Scott Kempner, I've come to know better because of the conversations included here. And then there were those I was meeting for the first time, like Matt Berninger from the National. All of these conversations were funny, moving, illuminating, validating. Springsteen is an artist who means very different things to different people. It helped this book when I could see Springsteen reflected in the eyes of his fellow songwriters and record makers.

Many are the people who at different times in my life have listened and let me rant and suggested alternatives and shown support. The list includes, in no particular order, Garth Brooks and Trisha Yearwood, who deserve a heartfelt thanks as a source of both friendship and inspiration, Amy Li at Crown, who worked on this book from its early stages and offered meaningful commentary and direction, Julie Flanagan at ICM, who has been a help to me over a period of years now, my students at NYU, the aforementioned Peter Guralnick, Mitchell Froom, John Biguenet, Scott Robinson, Brad Jones, Ward Just, Daniel Tashian, Angelo Petraglia, Kat Schaufelberger, Richie Joyce, Kate Fenner, Sayra Player, Ken and Anna Zankel, my mother, Hope Zanes, my sister, Julia Zanes, my niece Anna Zanes, my nephews Isak Saaf and Olaf Saaf, Paula Greif, Paul Muldoon and the members of Rogue Oliphant (David Mansfield, Cait O'Riordan, Chris Harford, Ray Kubian), the late and deeply missed Tom Petty, Mark Hurwitz, Stanley Booth, Bill Flanagan. Eric Ambel, Phil Galdston, Bob Santelli, Rob Weil, Jeff Hochberg, David Michael Kennedy, and Brother Cleve, who somehow got the Del Fuegos into a lot of trouble while also keeping us out of the worst of it. No doubt this list is incomplete, so forgive me for the names I've missed.

Jamie Berthe gets her own special mention in these acknowledgments. Her way of being in the world helped me to find a better one for myself. In that complicated tangle of jobs, ideas, families, dogs, guitars, children, recovery, socks, shirts, and pants, she has a way of seeing it all clearly and in some kind of order, a constellation rather than a car wreck, laughing at both the madness and the beauty. Her presence helped me bring this book home.

When writing about Bruce Springsteen, one hopes that an interview with the man himself might become possible. I told Gillian and Sloan that I had no special pull in that area but that I know someone by the name of Thom Zimny. I was the writer on Thom's film *The Gift: The Journey of Johnny Cash,* but my working relationship with him went back more than a decade. It was Thom who introduced me to Jon Landau during the making of *Elvis Presley: The Searcher,* for which Jon acted as producer, Thom as director, and I was among the interviews. Jon was my first stop for this book.

At the end of our initial session, Jon said he'd ask Bruce to consider speaking with me. No promises. Jon's belief that perhaps I was onto something, and the resultant message to Bruce, got this book under way. Chuck Plotkin, Toby Scott, and Al Teller all offered their time, recollections, and insights. Their contributions were crucial. A few years prior, I'd done an interview with Steven Van Zandt for the PBS series *Soundbreaking,* an interview Barbara Zadina allowed me to use here. *Nebraska* was such an intimate affair, few were the people closely involved. They showed up with dignity and kindness, giving important accounts.

When Jon Landau called me to say that Bruce was willing to talk, it was days away from the COVID lockdown, March 2020. Everyone was trying to figure out what it all meant, how to shop, what to clean, if you could make hand sanitizer from bourbon. I quickly knew the interview would have to go on pause. Then, each time we returned to scheduling, history intervened. George Floyd's death triggered protests, and I was out there with my sons. A siege on the Capitol did it again. Since the guy I wanted to interview was Bruce Springsteen, every time shit went down in the world, he got other calls he had to take. I watched him perform for a new president's inauguration and do a podcast and book with another president. At several turns Bruce reached out to Jon Landau saying, "Can you connect me with Warren Zanes to do the *Nebraska* interview?" Then Jon and the very helpful Mary Mac would line something up. Finally, one year later, I was in Colts Neck. Bruce has been a remarkable friend to this project, in so many ways its heart and mind.

I find more often than not that when I'm writing, I'm talking to my sons, Lucian and Piero. In putting some words down about *Nebraska,* this was certainly the case. I always hope they know art is there for the making. It's sacred, but it sure isn't out of reach. *Nebraska,* in its own way, was, yes, a little like the

Beatles on *Ed Sullivan,* a message saying, "You can do this." *Nebraska's* imperfections, its howls, its bent corners—none of it takes away from the power of the work. Quite the opposite. It reminds me, and I'm sure many others, that we shouldn't wait. The important thing is that you make it and mean it. If you have those two things covered, how "good" it sounds will matter far less. Because the how-good-it-sounds part is not what people are listening for when they really need a song.

Lucian and Piero let me talk about this album, about Bruce Springsteen and what he means to me. They let me insist on a few things, get a little emphatic behind the wheel or in the kitchen, at the dining room table and in the yard. Sometimes they pointed out the flaws in my thinking, at others approved, occasionally failed to listen at all, while mostly demonstrating patience and thought and a willingness to believe me when I talked about what art might be and do in their lives. I think they know how much I love them.

PHOTO: PIERO ZANES

WARREN ZANES is the *New York Times* bestselling author of *Petty: The Biography.* He played alongside Springsteen when he was a member of the Del Fuegos, and continues to record music, often with Paul Muldoon's Rogue Oliphant. Zanes holds a PhD in visual and cultural studies from the University of Rochester. He is a Grammy-nominated producer of the PBS series *Soundbreaking* and a consulting producer on the Oscar-winning *20 Feet from Stardom.* His work has appeared in *Rolling Stone* and the *Oxford American,* and he has served as a vice president at the Rock and Roll Hall of Fame and presently teaches at New York University.

ABOUT THE TYPE

This book was set in Bembo, a typeface based on an old-style Roman face that was used for Cardinal Pietro Bembo's tract *De Aetna* in 1495. Bembo was cut by Francesco Griffo (1450–1518) in the early sixteenth century for Italian Renaissance printer and publisher Aldus Manutius (1449–1515). The Lanston Monotype Company of Philadelphia brought the well-proportioned letterforms of Bembo to the United States in the 1930s.